T0195920

Love, Lust, and Loss

A Book of Poems and Short Stories of Passion

CLAUDACIOUS SHAKESPEARE

Order this book online at www.trafford.com
or email orders@trafford.com

Most Trafford titles are also available at major online book retailers.

Print information available on the last page.

ISBN: 978-1-4907-6969-1 (sc)
ISBN: 978-1-4907-6971-4 (hc)
ISBN: 978-1-4907-6970-7 (e)

Library of Congress Control Number: 2016901695

Trafford rev. 02/11/2016

 www.trafford.com

North America & international
toll-free: 1 888 232 4444 (USA & Canada)
fax: 812 355 4082

Preface

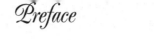

Throughout my life, I have had many loves.

I have been shown love. I've been heartbroken, I've broken hearts, and I've shown love.

I hope that the poems I write touch you, help you, and show you the ins and outs of love.

How great love can be, how much love can hurt, but also how much we can learn from love.

Sometimes we get so caught up in that one person that we close the doors to the ones truly meant for us.

Poetry for me is an expression of my life.

For me, the pen is my heart and mind and the ink is what's inside.

Writing is my way to pour out my feelings and what's on my mind and in my heart.

I think what makes me a good poet is the fact that everything I write comes from the heart, it flows, and it's from my soul.

Every aspect of life and every feeling in me I can relate to something else.

Putting it together in rhyme is hard sometimes, but letting it flow out of mind is what comes easy all the time (good thing not all poems have to rhyme, lol).

As you enter my world, my mind, my heart, my art…I hope that you find a piece of you within my work that allows you to open your eyes to a world within you that transcends you to a place and allows you to dream, love, remember and never give up on love.

———Claudacious Shakespeare

Table of Contents

Love

Lust

Loss

Short Stories of Passion

I pour my heart into all these words

Tears form in my wells as I think about each sentence

My heart bleeds for this writing

My heart beats for this writing

My hand cramps from this writing

But within me . . . within my soul

When I feeling a certain kind of way

Writing it out makes it better, it soothes me, keeps me chill

So I don't lose control

So for everything I feel . . . I fear . . . I get sad about or get mad about

I go to my outlet

My Pen

My Paper

My Thoughts

My Relief

My Therapy

My Writing

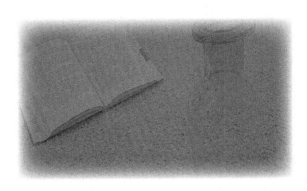

Affirmation of Me

I'm not the same me that I used to be

I've grown, I've learned, I trust myself completely

Not looking for love or another to complete me

All I need is GOD and HIS plan for my destiny

Roaming the earth, feeling like I didn't have direction

But once I gave myself to GOD, my mind became clear

and I loved my reflection

A work in progress that I still am

But with a mission, a vision, and a plan . . . no one

can stop me from being the best me that I can

8-4-11

The Dedication

This is dedicated to the special women in my life:

To my mother who gave me life

> Who raised me and taught me what's right

To my grandmother who instilled calmness while teaching me many things

> And inspired me to take flight

To my sister who always had my back

> Even though we used to fight

To the one who changed everything

> And showed me a new way of life

To the one who helped me "grow up"

> And showed me support for my dreams inside

> You came back again, loved me for me, so yeah, you get a third line

To the one that made me fall in love from a distance

> But kept me in line

To the one that was precious and held my love

> Forever deep inside

To the one that was new to the game

> But your family and mine are now forever the same

To the one that played with my mind

> Lead me to an illusion but unleashed my creative side

4

To the one that was like a butterfly

> Whose true beauty came out when she showed her love inside

To the one that opened up her heart and family

> Accepted me, loved me, and showed me how life could be

To the one that I love and watched grow

> Not only did it bring us closer it also allowed our love to grow

To you who taught me and opened up my eyes

> You showed me true feelings & love, the things people normally hide

To you that craves a love so true, a love you've never felt

> A love you're not used to, you've never truly felt my love, even when my love was waiting for you

To you, my love, the one I always think of

> Confusion, love and loss, life and lust, everything . . . done

Thank you, I love you. This is for you!

Thank You

To EVERYONE that helped me bring this dream of mine to life, I want to thank you. It has taken me years to put this book together. My words mean so much to me, so for my family and friends to help me bring visualization to my words is like a dream come true. You ALL gave my words life! This thank you is for you: D. Soto, R. Stevens, J. Morgan, P. Ivy, K. Abraham, B. Tate, C. Laws, D. Davidson, C. Agee, T. Sanders, B. Brown.

THANK YOU!

LOVE...

"In life and in love we go through ups and downs. This chapter tells stories of all the trials of love, the ups, the downs, and the in between."

What You Have Done

What you have done

Is open up my doors

They have been shut for so long, now it's time to explore

What you have done

     Is show me

          That there's more in life to see

               So I open my eyes and see things differently

What you have done

     Is give me hope

          When I thought I was lost

          When it came to love

               You showed me that if I

followed my heart

                    I could do things, I

always dreamed of

Vous êtes mon âme (You Are My Soul)

There's a special someone who has captured my soul

My Mind Body and Heart I cannot control

So deep that words can't even express

The way that I feel is something I can't repress

Your beauty is so . . . I can't let you go

Gorgeous on the outside, but I was speaking of your soul

To be high every day . . . without weed or ecstasy

That's how I feel when I talk to you . . . I can only imagine when you're next to me

A spell you have cast . . . a true work of art

Bet you didn't know you had captured me . . . right from the start

Some say love at first sight . . . but have you ever felt it in your soul?

It's lost when incomplete . . . but Luv you have made it whole

What Can I Say

What can I say

You have made my day

Just to see you

Though you don't look my way

I want to approach you

But what can I say

I'm at a loss for words

But I can't turn away

In the back of my mind

I would always wonder

What if you spared me your time

That's something I don't want to ponder

So I will step to you

With hopes, that you'll give me a chance

What can I offer you, you say

I can offer you true romance

Real and True

Real Love

I know that it's real

Cause of the way you make me feel

True Love

I know that it's true

You show me with the things you do

In Love

I long to be with you

I'm in deep, cause I truly love you

What Matters

Is the fact that you're my love

You are always there for me

And you're all I think of

I can't seem

To get you outta my head

Whether it's a vision of you

Or repetition of words you said . . .

My Love

That's what you are

More than just a person I've grown to love

More than just someone I always think of

You're my real love, my true, my Love!

Say It Again

Once is not enough

So say it again

I like the way it feels

When you say it again

Just hearing it gives me chills

So say it again

It soothes my heart and my soul

When you say it again

I start to lose all control

When you say I again

So one more time for the road

Baby, say it again!

I Love You!

My True Love

Though in a full room
Feels like just me and you

Captivated by your eyes
And our love is so true

To hold your hand, is just enough
To smell your scent, it sends a rush

I try to control my deepest feelings
Forever is just a word, unless it is with you I'm spending it

Given a gift of your love that is true
Knowing no one makes me feel as you do

Dare not to find someone else to take your place
Etched in my heart, your love will never be erased

Love Me

So often we want to be loved, craving love, needing love

I have love, your love, that love, her love, our love

Taking it all for granted

So often we look for love, those who want to be loved, I'm that one, I've wanted to be loved

You give me that love; she tries to give me that love

I gave that love . . .

That love was taken for granted, so I took that love back . . . it was mistreated, misguided

She wants it back, but now it's yours and your love I'm about to lose . . .

Oh how the tables turn, oh how we gain and lose love . . . but what's that true love?

That unconditional love, love you give, the love you say you want to take away

But if it is true, can it be given so easily and so easily taken away from you?

"Love me, love me now, love me in a special way"[1] . . . the words, the words to this song

So deep, drilled, etched into my head as the words are sung, "LOVE ME NOW GIRL, LOVE ME NOW! WHY don't you love me"[1]

---

[1] Written and produced by El DeBarge and recorded by R&B family group DeBarge, released on the Gordy label

It's not a question, I do love you, you don't have to ask . . . you don't have to demand, the love is here

The love is clear; just make sure you don't give my love away, because my heart, you see, my heart is here to stay

Can you love me through the good, through the bad, through my faults, when I make you sad?

Because regardless of it all, I love you, I love you in that special way, the way that no one can take from me or you . . . because the love we have is bound tighter than any type of glue . . . infused never to be parted . . . Love . . .

Love me in a special way . . . that's how I love you . . . so LOVE me NOW

In a Year

Lots of things can happen in a year

You could find new love there

I could find new love here

In a year

The one that you're truly meant for could be right in your face

Or in another place

But in a year

Who's to say they're the one

They could piss you off

Or they could totally fuck up

In a year

I know where my heart is now

It doesn't matter if you're ten or ten thousand miles away

I know my heart will stay the same toward you

No matter what you do

So, in a year

I'm going to keep pursuing you

And going to school

And keep doing what I must do

So in a year

I can come be with you

Share my dreams with you

And continue loving you

Throughout the year

Heart, Mind, Body, and Soul

When I talk to you

I seem to let it all go

I can't control myself

Sometimes I say stupid things

Well, there goes my mind

But I'm glad you're not a dream

My heart starts poundin'

When I look up at the screen

And I see your name in bold letters

And the star next to it has a gleam

Every time my phone rings and I hear "Für Elise"

My body gets weak

And I can't wait to hear you speak

The sound of your voice,

It soothes my soul

You bring out things in me

That I used to withhold

I want you as my lover

But more importantly as my friend

That's how we started out

And IF things don't work out, that's how it should end

Essence of a true woman

And yes, your Love is Golden

Strong, with the ability to carry twice your weight

I know you are an independent woman

But can I take you away

Twice your weight and twice as strong

Give me your burdens; here, I have a shoulder you can lean on

To have so much in common is one thing

But to take me to a level unseen is a completely different thing

I have to hold back; but I want to let loose

Go with the flow; give it time

If it's truly meant, then she will be with you

A heart of gold, because your love is golden

A treasure I would hold, embrace, never replace

For your gold is priceless, nothing could take your place

I want to build with you . . .

Draw a sketch of what it can be

We can then build our foundation . . . our friendship

As time transpires and the foundation is strong

We'll sculpt and paint, then show the world our love

Then sit back in awe of what we have . . . true and real love

Damn, I Love You

From heaven you were sent . . .

Our true love definitely meant . . .

So out of my mind, you got me spent . . .

Damn, I love you . . .

Got my back when I need you . . .

Holdin' it down as you always do . . .

Damn, I love you!

Sexy, you know it . . .

That good love, you show it . . .

Other ones try to get a foot in . . .

But don't even bother, compared to my baby . . .you'll never win

Slick wit' it, sayin' let's be friends . . .

I'm not dumb . . . not about to let you in

And ruin what I got with my baby . . .

I don't think so . . .

Lessons learned from the past . . .

There's no need for her to get in my ass

I've grown up, I know what I have

Sexy, Independent, Caring, Loving, Beautiful, Intriguing, Mindful, Spectacular, Extraordinary

Baby . . . that's you

Damn, I love you

Full potential has come and gone

Drawn out with a thin line

Approaching me are the young ones

Those of true maturity cannot be found

Prisoner of lust, yet guarded by love

Mixed emotion, confused there of

Lost within a soul, which doesn't want to be found

Confused by the ones who seem profound

Desperate, yet I search, but I must let go, hoping to be found, but I'm still forever yours

---

You give me so much love, so much crazy love, so much joy . . . tears of happiness, tears of love . . . missing you when we are apart, loving you because you have my heart, feeling your love even when you aren't here . . . knowing you love me . . . mmmm knowing you love me . . . you give me love, so much love, crazy love . . .

Up late, thinkin' . . . thinkin' about you.

Body sore, mind tired . . . yet all I can think about is you

Those sexy eyes, that beautiful smile, everything about you drives me wild . . .

Hmmmm

All I can think about is you

The things you do

The way you love me

No one compares to the way you oohhh.

But I'm not gonna go there

What happens between us is only for us to share

Except our love, I want to share it with the world

Let the world know, that you are my girl

So much on my mind . . . in life sometimes we search for love . . . sometimes love finds us when we stop looking . . . sometimes the love that is meant for us we are blind to, blinded by lust for another . . . lust can have your mind twisted, making you think it's love when it's not . . . don't mistake loneliness for love, then you will settle . . . don't look for love because you are lonely, let it come to you . . . if it is true love, you will know. You'll give your heart because your happiness is their happiness even if it isn't with you . . . love hurts . . . but if there was no love . . . if there was no love . . . hmmmm

---

As I head to lie down and close my eyes,

Will I dream of you, will I dream of our life?

Will I bask in the wonder of our future together?

Will God bless me to see another day?

So that I may be blessed to spend my life with you forever . . .

So Let's Say It's

So say it's love, love or lust

Trust, misguided

Misunderstood

Not known, what should I do

Lost, lost and confused

Wondering if you can tell me

What is the truth

Lost behind eyes, lost behind words lost behind kisses lost behind verbs

Wondering where the truth lies

Am I true to myself or do I surround myself with lies

Uncover my eyes

Let me see

What I thought was real

Is not meant to be

But the love I have for you so real

I know that it's real . . . I know how I feel

Forever

Baby, you got my mind spinnin'
Shit, you had me from the beginning

Girl, I love you so much
Damn, I can't wait to feel your touch

Not only a Goddess in the bed
But you've gotten in my head

You're the ruler of my heart
Damn, I hate that we are apart

Girl, I need you in my life
I wish that I could make you my wife

You know you mean the world to me
I was blind to true love, but now I can see

And my love for you can only grow

The deeper it gets, the more it shows

My love for you will never fade

I will always love you until my dying day

That kiss . . . your soft lips, those lips I miss . . . more than just bliss.

Your kiss in itself is pleasure . . . pleasure beyond measure . . .

Just to sit here and think, think about all the kisses that I missed playing the fool and letting my chance to feel your lips slip though my grasp and fall to the wayside . . .

But never again, never again will I miss your kiss . . .

The kiss that I long for when we are apart, the kiss that I miss . . .

The kiss from the lips that were meant . . . only . . . for . . . my . . . lips . . .

Your kiss . . . that kiss

Some Kind of Way

Usually, hearing your voice makes me feel some kind of way

A good feeling, a loving feeling, a feeling of all good things

A feeling that is great

But this time when I hear it

I feel some kind of way

I feel let down

No smiles, just a frown

Feeling sad and let down

Not used to feeling this kind of way when it comes to you

Still feeling some kind of way

Wishing I didn't feel this way

Wanting this feeling to change

Hoping you feel my pain

Hoping you want it to change

Needing you to step to me

Needing you to set these negative feelings free

Wanting to go back to how it used to be . . .

Feeling some kind of way

Praying this feeling will change

I love you so much

Please help me feel the right kind of way

The Heart Wants What the Heart Wants

Two plus two is four

My heart, their hearts, and yours

Caught up in the rapture of love

Engaged in a way some only dream of

My love, your love, her love, their love

Trapped in thoughts

Lost in dreams, hoping reality can set them free

She loves you, you love me

I love her, in love with me she will never be

The heart wants what it wants

Mine longs for a place to be

Given away to so many before, losing pieces as I walk out the door

My happiness is my biggest concern

Your happiness you deserve

Each person selfish in their own way

We want what we want, what others want is only hearsay

To change who I am is to love someone else

If you don't want the true me, then you love someone else

Communication is the biggest key

Open your mouth, talk to me

Tell me your thoughts; they won't fall upon deaf ears

Just be real with me, let's keep the air clear

If I want one thing and you want another

Let's part ways; we can still have love for one another

And just because she is ready, it may not be for you

The heart wants what the heart wants and it may not be you

It may not be me

Yet we stay tangled in this web

Afraid to hurt someone, no words said

The longer we wait, the deeper it gets

And no one can live the life they truly want to live . . .

Dreams

Every time I close my eyes, I dream of you, I dream of me

I daydream when the sun is out

I live in a world of dreams

I dreamt of having a life partner, someone to share my life with

I dreamt of having children, someone to share my dreams with

I dreamt of having fortune, a fortunate life living comfortably

I dreamt of you and me, the life we can have together

The love that we can make

The life that we can share

The kisses that you give me

The children that we raise together

The house that we make a home . . .

The constant smiles, the happiness

I dream, I dream, I dream

I close my eyes, I see you, I see me

I dream, I dream

I see our family, how happy we can be

I dream

I love you, you were meant for me

I dream . . .

That Love

That love

My love

Her love

Is undeniable

Unlike any other love

Unlike anyone could love

Nothing can touch her love

Unsure of some things

But not when it comes to love, my love, her love, that love

What kind of love . . .

Undying, unchanging, everlasting, that spoil-me love, unconditional, have-my-back love, understanding-me love, that speaking-at-the-same-time love, sharing-my-thoughts love, reading-my-mind love, send-chills-down-my-spine love . . .

That Love

1 a.m.

1 a.m. . . . . sitting here, wide awake, thinking about you

Knowing I can't go to bed next to you, I don't want to go to bed

So I stay . . . I stay awake . . . thinking . . . thinking about you

You see my heart has four chambers, but it's not the blood flow that keeps me going

It's the grace of God and knowing that my future holds you and I

Coward . . . that I may be, you see I try so hard to be the lion that I should be

Now 1:25 and awake I still am . . . watching a movie . . . alone . . . mad because I know where I should be, yet I'm stuck where I am

The easy way out, the road most traveled . . .

That's what others would do, and it seems that's the road I'm traveling

Yet I need to pave my own way, plan my future, not live in yesterday, because today you see is when my life's door opens

Because you hold the master key, the key to my heart, the key to my soul

I need you and your encouragement to help my life to unfold

I can't continue on this road that I'm traveling for it leads to uncertainty, regret, and . . .

Disappointment, disappointed, in myself; yes, I am . . . a good woman, a great woman

Afraid to lose you; yes, I am . . .

Without you, my heart would stop beating, my lungs would no longer fill with air . . .

1 a.m. I sit . . . 1:49 am still sitting here . . .

Breathless

The Thought	Me Breathless
Of You	You came
It Leaves	To Me
Me Breathless	I stood
Your eyes, your smile, your hair	There Breathless
Breathless	Never thought
To hear	You'd come to me
You speak	I'm Breathless
It leaves	

(Sometimes we go places and that one person will catch our eye. So magnificent, breathtaking, gorgeous . . . they leave us breathless. As we stand there, we often wonder, did they see me? Did they notice me looking their way? How do I approach them? What do I say? This poem is for that moment when they come our way. That moment that leaves us Breathless.)

Pure

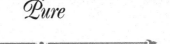

Our first kiss
Our first touch

When you look in my eyes
When I look in yours

The touch of your hand
The smell of your scent

A late-night talk
A good-morning kiss

An exchange of rings
An ocean of emotions

My love for you
Your love for me

The fact that you and I will always and forever be
The fact that our love will last for eternity

LUST ...

In life people come in and out of our lives. They all serve some sort of purpose. Some are here to love us, some were sent to teach us lessons, and some are here to simply satisfy certain urges. In comes sin . . . those bad, bad thoughts . . . Lust . . .

The Echo

Hello, hello, hello

How are you doing today?

Great, I'm fine as well . . . as well . . . as well

There's a question I want to ask you

Would you allow . . . would you allow . . . would you allow

Me to please you . . . please you . . . please you

All night . . . night . . . night

Long . . . long . . . long

Can I kiss you . . . kiss you . . . kiss you

Can I lick you . . . lick you . . . lick you

Can I touch you . . . touch you . . . touch you

I promise I'll be gentle . . . I'll be gentle . . . I'll be gentle

And I will not waste your time

From the time I start to the time I end . . . time I end . . . time I end

You will enjoy being mine

And you'll want it again . . . want it again . . . want it again

Release

Skin so soft

Lips to match

Kissing your breast

Caressing your back

Longing for you daily

Your taste lingering . . .

Pin me down

Ride me hard

Bite my thigh

Tie you down . . .

Kiss my neck

Wrap your tongue around my . . .

Release . . .

Release my ocean

As I drown you in my love

You let go, as you release

Your river flows . . .

Love, making love, connecting on another level

Sex, flex, sweat . . .

You want it, you dream of it, a dream come true

So hot when I lay you down and do you

My dreams come true when I do you

My Turn

-Close your eyes and take a deep breath

-I'm about to do things guaranteed to get you wet

-There's no doubt in my mind that you're the dominant one

-But tonight it's my turn and I'm gonna have some fun

-As much as you want to touch me, you can't do that

-I know it's taking everything to keep you holding back

-A fire burns inside you as you long for my touch

-Last night we were fucking, so tonight there's no rush

-I will tempt you, I will tease you, I will love you, I will please you

-I will lick the spot that makes you hot

-I will suck your nipples and give your clit a little tickle

-I'm gonna send chills down your spine

-Have you telling me, "You're mine!"

-Then as I kiss you upon your neck

-And run my tongue down your back

-Put my hands between your thighs

-Who needs a bed, we're doing just fine

-Heavy breathin'

-Lots of moanin'

-Making love, until the mornin'

-A bite here

-A squeeze there

-The smell of sex is in the air

-And now, I step down

-And I become the submissive

-Your Queen has the floor

-And yeah, I'm ready for some more!

Flesh

Burning desire to touch one's flesh, you call out a name with no discretion or stress

Eyes so deep, I swim within

My flesh to your flesh, you cum within

Confusion arises as you look in my eyes, are you being deceived

Your mind wonders why

The sex to be determined, no longer so true

You reach for comfort and love, not what you are used to

Strong as an ox, pushing deep inside you

Yet touching your spot as your rock can never do

Curiosity flows as you fight back the tears

It's not right you scream out as you draw them near

Look me in my eyes and tell me what do you see

Past the confusion, past the feelings, do you really see me

Not meant to be, I've done right for so long

But your flesh makes me cum in ways I've never known

Don't touch me, but wait, let me close my eyes

Let me sit back and imagine you going inside

So gentle with your touch, but rough when needed

Always touching my spot, for so long I've heeded

Should I give in, I ask, but the words cannot come out

Is it because I like it, or because your fingers are in my mouth

So I suck and grab as I push you

You stab, no longer sex that is drab

Against the wall or a double cab

Fire burning, sex I'm yearning, wet and turning over the flesh

Sweat we taste, don't stop the pace

Yet another place, I am such a disgrace

I feel bad for what I do, I feel bad for how I see you

You made me cum, like no other, whether a sista or brotha

Sex doesn't matter when I'm with you

Your flesh takes me up, to the highest peak, and brings me down into a deep sleep

Curiosity

Often trapped in a place that no one tends to go
We venture in our mind places that we don't want to show
Curiosity takes over, as it can tend to do
But do we go there or repress and take on deep issues

You live only once, so you should live life to its fullest
I'm not saying to sin, but when you pray ask for forgiveness
There will always be things that you can't be held accountable for
It's those moments of insanity that make life worth living for

Take that walk on the wild side as you know you want to do
Take a sip of that drink, let go of your inhibitions
And let your free will guide you

Now, I impose a dare, you can take it or spare
Yourself of your deepest thoughts, no one ever wants to go across
You might find yourself lost, or asking how this could be
That something that feels so good can be so bad for me

No drugs, no drinks, but this can get you high

Take you to another place, all the way to cloud nine

Allow the release of frustration, proven pleasure

You could never measure

Set back in motion, like a swim in the ocean

Feel the water as the breeze hits you

Cold to the touch, but my body heats you up

Now let me warn you, this is difficult for some people

A line never crossed, you believed only one type of person could please you

Use Me

Use me for your guilty pleasure

Tie me up, spank me with leather

Dress me up, come over, and tease me

All these things you do will please me

Sex me down, I'll sex you up

Against a wall, make love or fuck

Sexy attire, we both perspire

The sex is wet and I'm taking you higher

Use me, abuse me, tie me up

Spank me, bite me, I love to suck

Your breast so soft and nipples tender

Bite them, suck them, I'll be gentle

Walk in the room, hell yeah, I'm staring

You're wearing red heels, nothing else, eyes glaring

Over your way, heart racing, getting hard

You know what that means, you have been forewarned

So use me, spank me, tie me up

This is just the beginning

Can you hang or do you give up . . .

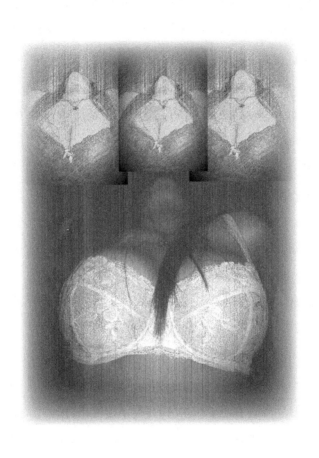

Quick Flows 2

To Be With You

Pulsating, yearning, hot, burning,

Desire, wanting, touching, haunting

Shiver, no quiver, wet, I taste

Inside, deep kissing, complete

Not yet, begging, more, sweating

No time, yet world spinning

Penetrate, ooh I can't wait

Can't stop, I dare not, climax

Once again, ten times, feels like a sin

Over the top, again we go

Take a deep breath, slow down,

Let's go

Take my hand, let me feel

You're so wet, is this real

Close my eyes, take a peek

You're bent over, I love pink

Wrap your legs around my waist

Whisper in my ear, touch my face

56

Kiss my lips, I'll kiss yours

Slide a finger in, listen to you moan

Keep it going, I know you'd like that . . .

But you only get a taste of what I can do

The real comes later . . . remember, patience is a virtue

The fire and desire, a look that can conspire,

penetrate and make you perspire.

After long hours, take a cold shower,

after I devour your sweet nectar

that comes from your flower!

It's Like That

Sexual, Sensual, Love Uncovered

Touch, Feel, Taste my lover

Warmth, Chills, Scratches on my back

Swollen, Sweat, Makin' love to you

Is Like That

Freaki~Azz~Pisces, do my eyes deceive me

A true freak in front of me

Tell me, do you feel me

Desire comes over me

Baby, cum and grind me

Lick you down your spine please

From yo neck 2 yo behind please

Turn the lights down low see

You Freaki~Azz~Pisces

Strawberries and whipped cream

Tell me your fantasy

Do you while you do me

69, do you feel me

Freaki~Azz~Pisces

Let me set you on fire

Body burning with desire

When you come near, I perspire

Cause your heat got me burning

Better yet, you got me yearning

Mind turning, no concerning . . . 'bout folks that are around

Right here in the park

Girl, let me lay you down

Or place your azz on the car

Eat your pussy like an all-star . . . pro

Don't you know, I like it when you cum down my throat?

Do you want more?

Now let me explore every facet of your body

Finding spots and getting naughty

Wild

Who can touch you like me

Spread your legs and get in between

Make you moan, like no other

Not just your friend, but a damn good lover

Looking in your eyes

You yearn for more

Calling my name

You beg for more

Your love is wet

Sweat is flying

Legs in the air

You scream like you're dying

Dying for me to cum inside

Feel my passion flow inside

Clench my back

Beg for a ride

Bend over now

Show me your freaky side

Fast and wild, fuck and suck, lick and stick, come and cum

Close your eyes and picture this

Picture me kissing your lips

Leaving you breathless as I touch your hips

Rubbing your body from your toes to your fingertips

Taking you places you've never been

Showing you things

Guaranteed to make your head spin

Picture this . . . me and you in a car

Hittin' the road, going places

Who knows how far

Then passion arises and fills the air

And even though we're on the road

We do things others don't dare

Shifting gears . . . going into sex mode

Suddenly pulling over on the side of the road

I'm on you; now you're on top

Licking, touching, kissing, sucking, biting, breathing, hot and wet fucking

People watching, but who gives a damn

When I'm with you, I'm in another land

As you mount my pride, I go deep inside

The pleasure you can't hide

As you thrust and go wild

I turn up a notch on my sex dial

Picture this . . . as you're about to cum

I lay you on your back

And proceed with my tongue

Deep, hot, deep, dripping, in and out

My fingers are slipping

You grab my head and squeeze with your legs

You try to push away; I grab your hips instead

You let out a scream

Fill my mouth with your cream

We get back on the road

As you pass out with sweet dreams

Throes of Making Love

Hypnotized by your eyes

Close your eyes as you grind

Fantasize as you ride

Open wide

I'll cum inside

Bend you over, kiss your back

Lean you against the wall

I know you like it like that

Call my name as I hit your spot

Tell me, Baby...

Are you hot?

Feel the sweat

As it hits the floor

Now it's time for my tongue to explore

Spread your thighs as I kiss your lips

Do you like it, when I lick your clit?

You're about to cum as you scream out more

So I won't stop till it's half past four

Dig your nails, deep in my back

Hold me tight, yeah, I like it like that

Do you wanna fuck . . .

Or do you wanna make love

As for me, I wanna do all the above

Now give me some head at the edge of the bed

You like when I talk dirty

So, Baby, do like I said

About to take you around the world

Your knees getting weak; don't worry, I got you, girl

You start to tremble as I start to stick

Just hold on tight and take all of this dick

Take a sip of your love

As your body succumbs

We become one

In the throes of making love

Daydream

Sitting
Thinkin' 'bout ya
Thinkin' 'bout all the freaky things we do
When you climb on top
I lose my mind
Bend you over
Pull you closer
Press your body to mine

Amazed, in a daze
I feel like it's a crime
That two people . . .
Could feel so right
Together we connect
In the bed on the floor
Balcony, calling me
As you scream out my name
In a chair, over there
Your body's driving me insane
With the motion of your hips
As I flip you over
To the side
Take my time

In and out
As you ride
When you climb on top
I lose my mind

Man, I'm lost
In this daydream
Your body creams
As you think about the things that happen between me and you
Thinkin' 'bout all the freaky
Things we do
Kiss you here
Touch you there
You don't care
I'm so lost
In this daydream

LOSS...

In life and in love we go through ups and downs. This chapter tells stories of all the trials of loss, trying to hold on to love, trying to make it work, and letting go . . .

How hard is the transition . . . and can couples really go from lovers to friends?

The hardest thing to cope with when trying to make that transition is boundaries . . .

Can you call me without asking why I didn't answer on the first ring or why didn't I answer at all . . .

We seem to get stuck in that routine of "I wanna know" . . . but why can't we let go . . .

Why can't we stop calling first thing in the morning, why can't we expect for that person not to call right back or answer when we call . . .

Is it truly that hard to accept when your once love has moved on . . . and not necessarily to another person but to another stage or point in their life that doesn't include you two as a couple . . .

But merely as friends . . .

Hard

I love you so much, it's hard

It's hard not to touch you

It's hard not to kiss you

It's hard when lips that you miss turn away and dismiss the desire that awaits them

It's hard

It's hard to go on, it's hard

You sleep next to me, but I feel alone, it's hard

I know I'm to blame for the forsaken game that now feels lame, you don't love me the same, and it's hard

To keep on wishing, it's hard

To keep on wishing, it's hard

To turn away it's hard

Baby, don't go, please stay

It's hard, I yearn for you, but it's hard

Who can I turn to, it's hard

Open your heart, girl, it's hard

Please give us a fresh new start, it's hard

So open your eyes, let me give you a prize, what you desire inside, hit me, slay my pride, fight me, go ahead and cry

Break down what you feel inside, there's no other way to put it behind
unless you confront what's on your mind

It's hard

Let it out, baby, cry, it's hard

I don't deserve you, but I love you, thank you

Cause I know it's hard

Meant For Me

Everything fell into place

No questions asked, no love erased

Slowing down, taking it slow

It's hard to do when your love continues to grow

Someone brand new, yet something so true

Our love was not rushed, we both had trust

Intertwined as one, our minds in sync

You finish my sentences; we were always on the same wavelength

Conversations until the dawn

Looking into your eyes as I sang our song

Saying "I Love You" and forever we would last

Giving me your heart, letting me into your past

Your eyes lit up when I entered the room

My heart filled with love, hoping I could see you soon

Taking a chance, that's what love makes you do

Not thinking about the trouble that can amount from certain things you do

Giving our all, knowing there was no one else

Making passionate love, opening doors there of

Knocking down walls and barriers alike

Kissing your back throughout the night

My smile unseen by any other

So much love, no way to hide it from others

Quality time always spent . . . all the little things

To us is what was made sense

Pulled apart at the seams

Yet still connected by the thread

Starting to unravel, the love we had almost dead

But love like this never dies; it can only be buried deep inside

Once you've had this love, you know

I Love You, Baby, I hope one day that you will come HOME!

Let Go

You ask me time and time again why can't I let go

Easier said than done, my love, your love is oh so . . .

I can't just walk away from love I've never felt before

You make love like a lioness

You make my lion roar

I ask myself what's wrong with me

Why can't I let her go

You understand the little things and your catering is so oh...

You try to give the best to me

You give me all of you

I try to give you what you need

But I can't give you me . . .

The one true thing that matters most is what I can't give

So time rolls by and hearts and minds begin to dwell deeper in love

So letting go is the best thing, or at least what your heart deserves

I should set you free

A lion I am yet still a coward, your eyes just can't see

That letting go is hard for me; easier for you . . . it must be your thing

So you with tough skin, knowing I'll just hurt you again, decide to do the thing that hurts most

You let me go and walk out the door . . . dried tears

You do what you must . . .

You spoke the words of love using your art as a weapon, destroying all in your path

You used those that loved you and abused those that adored you, strapped with your AK-47, burying land mines and building your traps

In the jungle of the world like a sniper you stood, watching and waiting for your prey

The innocent, the meek, the nice, kindhearted ones were the ones you seek

Playing the smallest violin of sob stories you load you gun, after you suck them in with love poems . . . you torture them one by one

You laugh at the sight of the things you put them through . . . slowly digging your knife and pouring salt in the open wounds

Devious, mischievous, a mind full of madness . . . yet lost and uncertain a heart full of sadness

But then you click like a switch or the sound of your trap going off

You spring into action using a machete to cut down the ones blocking what you sought

Here you are, my prey . . . what do you like, what must I say

A vulnerable one . . . you seem, I will suck you dry and drain you using your dreams

I will speak all of the words that you want to hear; I whisper the things that will draw you near

I can make you fall deep under my spell; by saying I love you . . . I can tell if you have fell

Like a vampire with a single bite, I will suck till the last drop

You won't suspect a thing 'cause I will blind you with my wonderful thoughts

But your heart is mine, it is my toy, I will use it for my plan

Make you think that you will lose me; as I lay dying, you will feel my wrath

I need some money 'cause I'm out in the cold

I am sick; so you can't see me, not just yet, let me put you on hold

And now I lie here on my deathbed, miraculously I am better,

Who would have figured that?

But I was out of work, and I cannot feed my kids, can you help me

I'm feeling weak as is . . .

So one by one she continues to fire off shots

While you lay there dying . . . she smiles . . . she got what she wants

You will never find another one like me.

Words often uttered by the ex as they walk out the door.

But let me tell you why you NEVER want to find the next that's like your EX . . .

You'll never find another like me

You're right, I won't, but that's okay with me

You see, if I found another like you, me and her would not be

I'm not with you for a reason, so why would I want someone like you

I already had you, you weren't meant for me

So when I find the next . . . SHE won't be like THEE

Like you; no, instead she will be my dream come true

She won't conform to the things I dream of

Cause when she comes to me that mold she will already be made from

Not looking for another like you; if they were like you, they would be set up to lose from go

Nothing wrong with the make-up of you

You're just not meant for me, our love just wasn't true

Wasn't real or unconditional, if it was, when I gained weight you wouldn't diss me or

Make fun when it comes to the things I like, keep me home instead of letting chill wit' my people for the night

Unconditional loves to love me, shows me love, puts nothing above me

Raises me up, whenever I'm down . . . loves EVERYTHING about me, ride or die, and ALWAYS down

So the next time you think to say those words . . . You'll never find someone like me

Just remember, I'm okay with that 'cause I found someone like her

Why me

I never stood a chance

Oh how I love you

Who gives a fuck about romance

Damn, I'm no good

So what's the point of even trying

Every time I'm let down

Shit, it feels like I'm dying

Who really cares

But I don't live for the past

I live for the future, but I only see my past

My high expectations

Always get me shut down

A very shallow person

Maybe that's why I have a frown

Am I true to myself?

Shit, right now I don't even know

Maybe I should stop

And just put love on hold

Close off my mind

When it comes to certain things

And focus my mind on learning shit

And earning green!

Goodbye

A kiss on the forehead, a tear on the shoulder

Saying goodbye

So much harder than some show

Loving the way you love me

Loving the things you do

Having to say goodbye

Is something we felt we had to do

I don't want you to hate

I don't want you to cry

I just want you to love me

Hell, sometimes I don't know why

I think because it's different

Some things no one can understand

So you blow me a kiss goodbye

So sad, so sad, so sad

Your tears flow like a stream

My tears fall like rain

To part from each other

Some may think it's insane

Who knows what a perfect fit is

Who knows God's plan

Even though we say goodbye

It doesn't mean we will never say hello again

Since We've

Since we've been together

It's like . . . birds of a feather

You and I . . . flocked together

No matter . . . what the weather

We saw . . . Eye to eye

Gave everything . . . a try

Making . . . much love

As time . . . went by and by

So you grew, mad love

And I . . . had love for you

But you wanted so much of me

And my heart . . . wasn't free

You and I . . . couldn't be

So that made . . . your heart bleed

No longer . . . would it beat

To the . . . rhythm of you and me

But I can't . . . let you go

Too much . . . love for you so

I try. . . to hold on

Cause your force. . . is so strong

So what's next. . . between us two

Does this mean. . . no me and you?

Cause I can't. . . let that be

No more us. . . is hard to see

Do You Miss Me

Do you miss me

As much as I miss you

I know you'd never tell me

That's just a thing you'd never do

Do you think about me at night

As you lie in your bed, missing how I held you tight

I know I think of you . . .

You are always in my head

I've tried to let you go

But my feelings for you just aren't dead

I know you've moved on

So I guess there's nothing to it

But knowing your love was true to my heart

It makes it hard for me to allow you to part

But do you miss me

Is what I want to know

I wish I knew

I wish it showed

A fool in love

I am once again

I have no choice but to move on

This game of love, I will never win

So Good to Me

Find someone that will do for you
And not always you for them

Damn, you were so good to me

Countless days and countless nights
Full of lovin' and never fights

Damn, you were so good to me

Watching movies in my bed
Until the movies started watching us instead

Damn, you were so good to me

Cookin' food in the nude
You always kept my belly full

Damn, you were so good to me

Quiet walks in the park

Making love way past dark

Our song I sang to you

We did all the things true lovers do

You were so good, but now you're gone

Now I'm sitting here singing this sad-ass song

Damn, you were so good to me

Enough

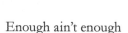

Enough ain't enough

Ain't enough

Not good enough, don't have enough, not enough

Not enough for you

So used to the finer things, the better things, being spoiled and treated

And I can't treat you like them, but I love you, so hmmm . . .

Say I'm enough, I'm good enough, I do enough, I have enough

But not good enough, so get enough from whom?

Not from me 'cause you see that I, me, I'm not good enough for you

No money, no cash, no *dinero*, no bread, no paper, no cheese, no you

You come here, say I'm enough, but you go to others for stuff, for stuff that I can't provide for you

So really enough ain't enough

Ain't enough

Not enough for you

My love ain't enough, not enough to hold strong, to hold on, to keep us stuck like glue

'Cause my feelings of inadequacy will make me want to run free

As you keep telling me these things, these things that people

These other people who aren't you and me, these people who do these things

These things that I can't do for you

So you dwell on the past and the things you once had, these things I can't give to you, Boo

But if one day you feel that my enough is enough

Is enough for you and for me

Then maybe that day you and I can say

That enough is enough

Just me and you

Played

Found a love, a love so true
Captured my heart, all things were brand new

Fell so hard, fell so fast
I just knew that it would last

Never thought that you could be taken
Played for a fool, I was mistaken

Fed constant lies all the time
A friend of yours, no friend of mine

Once my friend
Now we have no ties

There in my face
Though it happened over time

Woke up alone
You were there by her side

Still just friends, my nightmare begins

Your heart I had but pushed away

But I was told

You would never go away

Played for a fool, I was mistaken

No longer with me, the love you are makin'

Guess it's my fault, or maybe it's not

I used to be the one to get you hot

I must move along, that's what I'm always told

But late at night it's you I want to hold

That last little part was my confession

No choice I have but to chalk it up to a well-taught lesson

There is one for all

There is me for you

When I see you my heart starts to fly

But why?

Why can't we be?

Who is it that you wish to see?

For I know it is not me

Can we be together for all eternity?

For I can't live without you internally.

Inside me, within my heart

For when we part, it is broken like a fragile piece of art

You are my caretaker, you are my friend, you are my love, you are my pride, you are my joy,

You are

THE ONE

THE ONE I LOVE

THE ONE I NEED

THE ONE WHO I CHOOSE TO BE . . . WITH

So where did we go wrong?

Why must I sing this sad song?

This is just a pardon, because now I must harden

My Heart, now a solid piece of rock

Which once you held, until it fell, now I'm trapped in my own hell

A hell of loneliness, solitude, unhappiness.

Then this one question still remains

How can one, one person have such a grasp on another

No one will ever know; just remember this

When that person gives you that final kiss, don't let them go, make them hold on, make them see what they will miss, for you must be strong. And when they let you go,

Let them be the one who cannot stand. Why?

Because you have left them with your brand, your seal, your FINAL KISS!

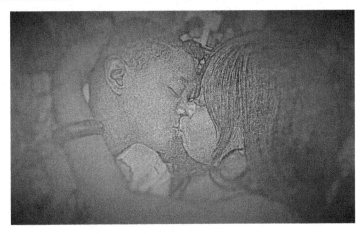

Short Stories Of Passion

I've always known that I wanted to be in love, I've wanted to be married, I've wanted a family, I've wanted to know that I had my one and only someone. It was a real love and true love for love. I didn't have a childhood lacking love, quite the opposite, I was shown love every day by my mother. Yes, it is true, my father wasn't around. He was always on the road, but my mother gave me enough love for the both of them. I remember being very young when I realized that the love I had inside me was a love that I wanted to share with someone very special. So let's travel back in time to when I was but a child.

I grew up in the suburbs. I never wanted much. I never asked for much, but my family always made sure that I was taken care of. I went to school, I made good grades, I listened to my parents, and I enjoyed time with my friends. Yes, I had my share of crushes. Being a young girl, my crushes varied. I never really truly revealed who my crushes were. I just kept them in my head. I had a crush on the cute young boy in class, you know, the one with the dimples, infectious smile, dark hair, charismatic. At the same time, I had a crush on my teacher. You know the little childhood crush, because seeing *her*—yes, "her"—made me just as happy as it did to see him. It wasn't like I wanted to be her or admired her. I thought she was beautiful. I liked her like I liked him, but of course I never told anyone. How crazy is it for a child in elementary school to have a crush on a woman? Once again, of course, I left all these thoughts to myself. It wasn't just a fly-by-night feeling. All throughout elementary school I was plagued with the emotions of liking the cute little boys and the beautiful grown women.

Finally, in middle school I went beyond my feelings that were in my mind. I had my first "boyfriend." You know, the guy that I would talk to on the phone, go to the movies with, and he'd walk me to class. That still didn't change the fact that I still had crushes on the beautiful women who were my teachers. I wasn't stupid. I would never do "too much." But I did make sure I was the best I could be in their classes and was somewhat of a "teacher's pet." I formed bonds and close relationships with those teachers and would do whatever I could to spend time with and around them. Of course, I would never reveal my real intentions. I don't even think I knew my intentions when I wanted to be close to those women. As for my boyfriend, he was a great guy and he was very sweet, but it was middle school. It's not like we were going to get married or anything. So we parted ways as we went to high school.

In high school, I experienced the same emotions. There were the guys that I had a crush on, but at the same time, there were those hidden feelings for my female teachers. Yes! Once again, me and those crazy feelings for my teachers. This time I actually went a tad bit further and more than just getting close to those teachers, I kind of showed these feelings, flirting here and there, gifts . . . and it's crazy because they accepted these gifts. Yet I still had no idea of the true feelings that lay within me toward them. Until she came into my life. She showed me something subliminally (and she wasn't a teacher but a peer). She gave me her number and showed me that there were other women—well, girls that liked girls. Yes, I liked boys, but for some reason as a teen as I sang in my room to the posters on my wall. The deeper emotions were for the female artist who I wanted to make my queen rather than the male artist, whom I never thought of being my king. Although she approached me and gave me her number, which I called, I still couldn't wrap my mind around the concept of there being a girl that liked me like how I like the women that I held in my mind. So I befriended her, we spent time together, got to know one another, and she taught me so much. I finally saw my chance to express my passion for love that I had held back for so long. Yes, it is true, I had boyfriends but I was too young to know what love was at that time. I mean, I cared about them, but who truly knows what love is when you are thirteen or even fifteen. Granted, I was only fifteen when this young woman came to me, but the feeling was so different from what it was when I was with a guy. It was like a connection, a bond, a love, a feeling, a passion. We spent every day together and we spent every moment that we could together. We wanted to get married. I was only sixteen and she was eighteen, but that's what we wanted. Never mind the fact that two women can't get married. That was never even a thought that crossed our minds or stopped us from exchanging rings and vows to one another in front of her best friend. So in our minds we were married. We even created our own marriage certificate that we signed and held each other to. Until she went away to college, and although I went to see her, the college life drew her in and the curiosity and passion for the unknown led her to experiment with other women and men. Which in turn lead me to build a bond with another woman.

Still on that search to find love, the passion for love that I so desperately needed to fill this part of me that wanted to give so much of myself to another, I, at a young age, gave my heart to many with the hope that they too would share in the love that I wanted to give. I even tried to make things work with my first love again. We moved in together after I graduated and everything—after all, we were still "married." I forgave her for her infidelities and she forgave me for my attempts at finding a new love to replace her with, and we tried. We tried for the better half of a year, until her wandering eye led her to yet another and that led me back to the one I went to before. I always felt like that woman loved me. And if she didn't, she still showed me things I never experienced, and I couldn't help but go back to her, I wanted more. There was something about older women that truly drew me in. So my "wife" did her thing, I did mine, and I spent time with my other woman whenever I could. Thing about that was, my other woman had someone at home. She just wasn't happy either. I didn't truly get the picture or opened my eyes until the night the three of us were together, and to my surprise, my "wife" and my other woman were together in an intimate way. They both said they did it for me, but neither realized when I was in a completely different room I couldn't watch. I walked away. I had to ask myself what am I getting myself into. I walked away from my other woman, I walked away from my "wife" and I tried to give myself a new start at love, begin a new life.

Curiosity always kills the cat, and my curiosity got the best of me when I fell for the sexy voice over the radio. No, she wasn't a radio personality but the dispatcher at my job. I intrigued her as much as she intrigued me, and all this passion within me led me to finally meet the woman behind the voice. I must say, when I first saw her, I was taken. I believe at this point in time love had worn me so thin that my initial thought process left and it was lust over love that drew me into this thing. She said the first time she saw me I looked at her as if I were undressing her with my eyes. Honestly, I can't say that I was, but I will admit I was looking at her supple breast, round ass, and luscious thighs. When I was young, it wasn't about sex. It was about the feeling of love. And when you give so much love only to be hurt, well, to bounce back it takes time. So in the meanwhile I let my lion's eye guide me and I was sure love would follow. We spent time, we learned each other, and you see, she had never been with a woman. I was her first, and I treated her like she wanted and needed. She seemed to have the "white knight" syndrome. She was in a bad situation and she wanted to be rescued from it. Me, being the kind-natured person I was, wanted to rescue her and show her that she deserved something better. The time we spent and the love we made was incredible, every aspect of it, and I treated her like she was the queen that I so badly wanted. She took care of me and I took care of her, but still being so young, I didn't fulfill ALL of her needs. Here I go again with an older woman, a woman whose needs stretched beyond herself, but she also had smaller loves in her life that needed her and needed me. I thought I was ready because this was the family I so badly craved. We got a place for our family and lived together happily. Or so I thought until the stresses of life took over and love wasn't strong enough to keep this union from unraveling because I was everything a spouse was but not a parent should be. I loved her and her children and I thought I was doing my best, but the arguments told otherwise and the arguments led to more stress. And the stress led to nights alone—me and the kids, she didn't come home. First one night, then a week. Next thing I know, I'm completely alone, just me, four walls, this bed, and these sheets. Until she crossed the line and disrespected me and our house and what we built. She walked away from me and started a new life but still wanted me for my skills. The love I had for her made me carry on and do things even though I knew it wasn't right. Why would I sneak over and sneak in when you left me for her and started this new life? Again, my passion for love because I just knew she was "the one." It was so hard to let go that depression set in and it would be a year before I would try to love again.

When I got my head right, I tried again and met someone that was sweet and true; however, she was younger than what I was used to. Again, spending time and getting to know one another. This would prove to be the longest relationship that I have had with a woman (well a steady relationship without breaks that is). No other people, just me and her, and we dated and we had fun. We waited before getting a place until it was time and were sure of this together thing. Things were good, but then I expected too much. See, being with older women, there's a certain home environment that you are used to, that you begin to expect. See, if I'm playing the role of the "breadwinner," then I expect you to play the role of the . . . well, you know. I know that we were equals and we could both do the same, but sometimes when you do a bit more, you would hope that the person you love takes care of you the same. She was sweet and we tried. Ultimately, when it came to me and her, it just wasn't our time. We were never on the same page, and the last one did quite a number on me. It changed me. It made me constantly keep my "options" open. Always looking for the "perfect" one. So when there was trouble in paradise, I ran . . . well, I looked elsewhere really. Always looking for someone to fill the void I was missing in the current relationship that I was in. This was not a good trait, but for me, I thought it was a win. So I looked and I searched and I found other loves and the one that I found was unexpected, someone I never thought of.

See, I met this chick. I found her online, don't remember the page, but we chatted for some time. She was that type of girl that played to your weakness, realized what you like, and played it as her strength. See, she tried to get me to get her things, send her money, and go in on her ex. By that I mean, she wanted me to confront her ex and let her know that she had moved on to the next. The only thing I did that was worth the whole situation was when I went in on the ex. For some reason, when things went sour, something inside me gave me the power and the insight that told me to hit her ex up. We started to compare notes and things didn't add up, and from there we became kinda cool. Knowing that she had played both of us like we were fools. Then she told me about her ex girl and introduced me. Then what came next was me and her ex girl finding things in common too. Then those things led to another and I was trying to see her further, but at the time she was in another state. I truly wanted to meet her, but didn't want to take a chance. I found family there and knew this would justify my flying there, knowing I was really going for the romance, to see her, and see if what we shared was true. When I arrived, everything was pretty good and she was kinda sexy too.

There wasn't too much keeping her there, so I flew her here, I wasted no time there. She stayed with me, I tried to give her what she couldn't get where she lived previously. Help with a job and going back to school. I hooked my girl up, yet she played me like a fool. She found someone else that she was talking to online. But who cares anyway, my "lil sis" occupied my time. Crazy coincidence how we met and where she lived. When I took the ex home I went to see "lil sis" at her crib. Got to know her, had fun hanging out. Taught her some things she didn't know much about.

Then I came home upset about my ex. I left her alone and moved on to the next. Still searching online is where I messed around and found her. Didn't want a relationship, I just wanted to uh . . . pound her. Met her one time, watched a movie, then hit it, explained to her that I was moving and this would be it. She wanted to meet again, out drinking it was cool . . . smashed again, I got it in, I was no fool. I made plans to move and find a job in another state. Went on interviews, even looked for a place to stay. Came back home and saw her once again. She sucked me in with dinner and even invited her fam. A sucker for kids, I fell for her little girl. I came around more, next thing I know . . . all the sex became a relationship with her. So I stayed here and got a place with her. Next thing I know, three years have passed, my life was a blur. It was filled with traveling, arguments, and ass. So many things going on in my mind, and my passion for love is why I stayed tied. Despite gaining weight and depression outweighing the love. So unhappy at that time in my life and to think I considered making her my wife. The time, it did go by, and I felt like it was wasted. Well, I can't say it was wasted; for everything is a lesson and in this one I learned I can't give in to temptation. I can't fall for the one that gave it up but truly wanted more. Then let it go from a fling, to a thing, to a deep relationship . . . something I wasn't wanting. At least not from her at that time. I did no wrong in this thing (I never cheated). I stayed true to her.

I was her everything, but her insecurities are what pushed me away. She said I fucked her and her and her too, but the truth of the matter, I was only fucking you! I just needed to get out. Like a prisoner, I felt trapped in my life. When I hung out with friends, in her mind I was fucking. When I went to play ball, in her mind I was screwing them all. Even when I went to the store, in her mind, I was out being a whore.

I couldn't take it any more, so I vented to relieve some frustration. I vented to the one I felt I should have been with at that time. She gave me something precious and she thought she would be mine. I played our relationship off as less than it was because I was too old and to me she was so young. Not underage, but she couldn't even buy a drink; old enough to go to jail or join the army, but still too young for me. So I continued to call her my "lil sis" and we remained friends. Well, we were friends until she reached the age that in my eyes was old enough for my consent. Before I go into this new tale, I will just say the other one didn't prevail. I lied my way out and said I had to go back home. I needed an out. I could no longer live in that home. My mind was shattered and I was beyond depressed, so far from happy and completely and totally stressed. Love no longer lived here and there was too much anger. We parted ways and I moved on and was much, much saner.

Now back to this young love. I loss all of the weight I gained, dropped the 50 pounds that depression made me put on. It was great! Although she was in another city, I needed her love. We connected on levels no one could ever think of. She was so great to me and she thought I was her "ONE." She treated me like I was the only person that she had ever dreamed of. She said that she'd loved me ever since she could remember, and I loved her too. It was amazing, I remember. I flew her to me and she made my house a home. She was there for me and made right all my wrongs. Plans were made and I just knew this would last our lives long. Yet she wasn't ready for the life I wanted with her. She still longed for her family that was thousands of miles back home. So she went back home and then came back to me. The last time she went back, she took most of her things. It left me heartbroken and I felt like she was done, like she had given up on all the things we had begun. We were supposed to start a life but I guess I was looking for too much. She was still young and wanted to be near her mom, siblings, and such. I messed up a great thing, because I felt she didn't want me. I pushed her away and did my thing not knowing, that I was killing her heart slowly. I wanted to wait, but while she was gone, I ran into someone from my past.

A long-lost love, the older woman from the past. The one that got away, so to speak, is who she was to me. I was so young at the time and she had a few years on me back then. She said that she always loved me but never knew how to reach me again. It had been ten years since I last looked in her eyes. She had just got out of a relationship and so did I. Not looking for love, but at the time I was lonely. I felt like my girl walked away and didn't want me. I knew how I felt when it came to this woman from my past. I knew I loved her and she WAS a great piece of ass. I know it comes off wrong and I may sound like a jerk, but passion also lies in the way you put in work. When you lay it down and leave that stain on the mind, making someone wonder will it bring back the good ole times. With a night of passion, I had broken my young love's heart. We parted ways and I began a journey with my past . . . a new start.

I wanted a relationship and she didn't want labels. We were together for a year, living together, but no, I can't "claim" you. Little remarks like "you don't bring sand to the beach" or "let's part ways and see how many numbers we get each." Definitely not words of someone that's committed. I guess it was my own fault, I walked into it, I'll admit it. I thought it would be different. I guess I ask for too much, I'll admit it. She wanted the life, but she didn't want the title. I wanted them both, so again my mind went idle. Out for a show is how she and I met. I waltz to a woman and danced on her like we've already met. Jealousy takes over and here comes you, trying to stake your claim on the one that loves you. I realize this "friend" is someone I haven't met, but we exchange info and from time to time we'd chat. She became a true friend someone who is truly there for me. Has my back and cares for me completely. She doesn't come on to me or try to disrespect what I have. She keeps her distance, but a real friend is what I have. When I need someone to talk to, she gave me that ear, when I needed some advice, she didn't just tell me what I wanted to hear. She never sabotaged. She advised on what she thought was true, true to my heart and making things right with who I was going home to. Being a good friend and getting me out when I needed it, supporting me and having my back when she knew that I needed it. I was there for her as she went on different dates, looking for the one for her, trying to find her mate. It really wasn't her that made me decide to end what I had, it was the nights full of tears and begging for something I didn't have. All I wanted was commitment and to feel wanted by you. You can stick your finger down my ex's mouth but get mad when I try to gain support for what I do. You assume I'm getting numbers but I'm building my poetry base. That's something you wouldn't know. You never asked, you assumed. I'm not your ex! Babe! Late at night when I cried to you, I decided I couldn't do it. I needed someone I could commit to.

We parted ways, and yeah, I dated my friend. She made me laugh and she was amazing to me from the beginning. We took our time and we dated for a minute, then Christmas came and I asked you for commitment. You told me yes, and we were happy, I must say. Spending time, me and your family, you and mine, it was all great. All things that I wanted to do, but there was a part of me that was still bruised. A part of me that couldn't be fixed by love or by another person, only by the Man up above. See, that passion for love that I longed for I looked for in people. That's where my mistakes were made, that's what made my love lethal. Because she gave me love the best way she knew how. She was there for me and gave me all of her, no doubt. When I felt there was doubt and that she didn't love me the same, I looked for attention elsewhere, I was the only one to blame. So I let another in. She filled the space I thought was empty. All the things I knew I wanted, she came with it all, good and plenty. It was crazy how she read me like she was in my mind. She knew exactly what I wanted and how I wanted it every time. Crazy thing is my love left me, not once but twice. The second time, I let it be. I didn't try to come back because I had someone new in my life.

It's crazy, because when the devil comes to your door, he's not dressed in horns and pitchfork, he looks like EVERYTHING you ever wanted, EVERYTHING you are asking for. Not saying she was the devil, but temptation she definitely was, but I can't fault her for her intentions. Like all of us, she only wanted love. A love that she thought she could get from me and I thought I had, but for some reason when it came to her, the one thing I begged for, I couldn't give her, it was sad. I couldn't commit to her, the thing I longed for from others. It wasn't anything she had done. She was amazing, truly different from the others. Yes, I knew I did her wrong and I did fight for her love. However, when it came to her, once that shipped sailed there was no return.

Through my trials and tribulations, my true love stuck through it all. Although I brushed her aside, she fought for me and gave it her all. When I came to my wits' end and neither wanted my love, I hit rock bottom and wanted nothing more than to leave this earth. One came to me with her voice, the other a book. Although soothing and understanding, the book is what took over my life and shook my soul with just one look. The book led me to God and helped me learn to love me. Put Him first in my life and know that all other things would eventually fall into place as I continued to proceed. One took the pain I caused her and walked away. She shut me out as if the love we shared was nothing, it never existed, and it just went away. The other was there no matter how much it hurt. She prayed for and with me when I needed it. I pulled away from her because what I did was too much and she didn't deserve it. Neither of them did, I just wasn't a great person. I needed to be made over, starting off with the constant lies.

So for those of you who may be reading this, if a part applies to you, I think you know this and it may have given answers to your whys. If you see some things that you didn't know before, here is my confession to all the things you wondered about before. If you were curious whether I left you for whoever, read what I wrote and you can piece the clues together. I apologize for the lies and the pain, just know that God made me over and the person writing this is not the same. Not the same person whose passion for love was breaking hearts on a journey to find love. Once I found love in God and myself, I found that love would come to me once I stopped looking, and it has.

I'm not going to lie and say it was easy, because I still have to go on more journeys, journeys to find out that beauty is only skin deep and looking for love in the wrong place will still leave you lonely. So many people are hurt and damaged and don't know how to love or how to give themselves to someone that truly cares for them. It's remarkable, the only thing that came from these "flings" was maybe a friendship but nothing more, and I'm not sad. See, once again it opened my eyes to something I didn't see, something I never had. I will admit that at one time I felt that my deeper love surfaced again. But that love surfaced for someone that could be nothing but my friend. Without going too deep into this, I will say she captured a piece of my heart. And every time I laid eyes on her she knew what to do to melt my heart. Maybe afraid of what I had to give, she just could not give herself to me. So, sadly, I had to make a choice to walk away without knowing if there could ever be a her and me. So as time went on and I sat there alone, I came to a realization. That my true love I was searching for was always right in front of me and still loved me without hesitation.

To my real life "Cookie," you have had my back. You saw my vision when I was blind, you urged me to jump because you knew that I would spread my wings and fly. When I was down you lifted me up and you prayed by my side. You never held me back or spoke negatively of the things I pursued in life that you knew I held a deep passion for inside. You made me stick to my word, no matter what it was, you held me accountable for all things that I've done. You're the first to sing my praises and hold my heart next to yours. You get on me when you know I'm slacking, procrastinating, or worse. You have shown me what true love is, and ours will prevail. As long as we base all things in life on God and make Him the foundation on which we build.

You would think that was the end and that all these things held true. However, once a heart is damaged, it can transform you. I hurt you so deep and left a wound deep in your heart. No matter how hard you tried, you could no longer love me as you did from the start. You didn't trust me and the things I did, so you went looking for my lies. You searched and searched and you were so unhappy with the things that you would find. And although you love me, you could no longer subject yourself to that. So once again you let me go, but you're still by my side, I can vouch for that. A true friend and it always shows.

Each one of you still holds a place in my heart, some of us still talk, some of us have grown far apart. One of you has become my absolute best friend, you love me no matter what and deal with my crap, sob stories, love stories, and the love I fall out of and in. No matter who it is, in your eyes no one will ever be good enough. It's only because you love me and you want what is best for me. Thank you for listening and going through all my crap with me, you've known me the longest and you always come through. I can talk to you about anything and for that I love you.

Who knows what the future holds for me as I still have a passion for love. Maybe I will end up with someone from the past or maybe God will guide to me a new love. Either way, I must stop searching and realize that not everyone is perfect. It's about finding the one that loves me for me and I the same for them, and everything else, well, we can put the work in. We must pray together and have a solid foundation built on our faith in God. Fight for me and I will fight for you. Trust me and know that I love you. I know my faults and the things I do wrong, those things I now see, I promise I will work on. I know I'm not perfect, but I promise I'm trying. I'm taking things a day at a time. My passion for love will be matched, just not in my timing.

As I walked into her classroom, I noticed her smile. She looked at me with slight interest, a slight smirk, but friendly in a sense. Light brown eyes, very enticing. Flowing brown hair and dressed very nicely. A student, you ask, no, it was my instructor. As for me, I'm just the average Joe with an above-average grade point, 3.89 to be exact. Six feet even, athletic build (I work out at least three times a week), play football on my university's team, light brown eyes, low-cut black hair, clean shaven. This was my third year in college, and at the end of the spring term I will be twenty. I've dated plenty of women before and I've always noticed that I had a thing for the older woman; either that or a woman with a high maturity level. I know I seem to be young myself, but I've been on my own since I was seventeen, so I learned to grow up pretty quickly. I tried dating a younger woman and women my age, but they never knew how to "read" me or understand what I truly wanted and needed out of a relationship. Maybe that's what drives this insatiable desire for the older woman, the sex appeal, the intelligence, knowing what they want and what it takes to get it. That drive alone, what a turn on, and the way she carries herself alludes that she had it all.

Her legs bronze like an Egyptian queen and shaped as if she ran ten miles every day. Her short blue skirt and low-cut white blouse—very professional, but definitely made the mind wonder. Then she spoke . . . "Hello, class." Her accent, a familiar sound, it put you in the mind of the actress Roselyn Sanchez. She kind of reminded me of her as well. I've ALWAYS found Roselyn sexy. She then began to tell us her name, "I am Ms. Valencia De Leon and I will be your Spanish instructor." Not meaning to stare, but I could not keep my eyes off of her; I had to make myself known. So as class ended, I approached Ms. De Leon and introduced myself. "Hi, my name is Drake Hunter and I have been looking forward to this class all year." Of course, kissing up doesn't hurt either, right? "Well, Drake, I hope that you enjoy learning in my class as much as I enjoy teaching it," she replied. She smiled at me and I felt my collar around my neck start to burn. I had never had a professor this hot before.

I noticed that when I spoke to her she seemed younger than I thought, maybe her late twenties early thirties. I was so used to having professors that seemed like they had been instructing since the dawn of time. She was different and she definitely left a stain in my mind. As I headed back to my dorm, I found myself mentally undressing her over and over again and imagining the many things I would like to do to her.

Going to class these past few weeks had been like heaven. Not only is she a good instructor, but she is also definitely good eye candy. I made sure that I paid attention, and I couldn't have cared less about anyone else thinking that I was the teacher's pet. I answered every question she asked. Whether I was right or wrong or how stupid I sounded, at least she saw me trying, right? She learned my name in no time, but she only looked at me occasionally. However, I did love oh so much those smiles she threw my way. I always felt like there was something more between us, but of course, I didn't want to jump the gun. Maybe she was just being nice. Whatever it was, I enjoyed it and basked in it every moment I got. Who cares if my classmates gave me a hard time? I wanted to make sure she noticed me and that she knew that I noticed her.

Okay, so fast forward, let me take you to the day that I will never forget. Ms. De Leon was passing back our latest exam. I knew I aced this one. I studied my ass off. When she handed the papers back, I looked down at my grade. A D! What the hell! I never get D's! Ms. De Leon noticed the discontent on my face. She then bent over and whispered in my ear, "Can you stay after class? I need to speak to you about your grade." Pissed at my grade, I didn't know if I should be happy because I felt her breath caress my earlobe as she whispered to me and because she wanted me to stay after, or if I should be worried. Well, nonetheless, I stayed. What other choice did I have? I can't fail! After closing her door, she walked over to her desk and sat on top of it; a tad bit of her short skirt rose as she crossed her legs and asked me to approach her desk. When I approached her, she took the paper out of my hand. "Drake, you have never made a grade this low in my class before." Slightly leaning over, she finished by saying, "I'm worried about you." As I stood there looking into her eyes, everything she said went over my head, and all I could see was me bending her over her desk and kissing the back of her neck.

"Hello, Drake, are you listening?" she said as she noticed that I seemed to be distracted. "Oh, I'm sorry, Ms. De Leon. Yes, I'm listening," I replied. "Well, what should we do about this?" she asked. "Tutoring?" I answered. "Okay, that is definitely an option. You can either meet with the tutors that the school offers or I can tutor you privately after my last class of the day," she replied. Hmmm, now which should I choose? Sitting in a library with a group of students or time alone with Ms. De Leon? Obliviously, I'm going to go with time alone with the sexiest professor I've ever encountered. "I think it would serve me better if I see you after your class. I actually do better one on one with an instructor than I do in groups or learning from peers," I responded. She agreed to the meeting and asked if I could come back today.

When I returned to her classroom, I was a bit nervous. "Did you bring your book with you?" I pulled out my book and she began to go over the last thing covered in her class. She made sure that I understood the correct pronunciation and use of the diction. When she noticed me getting frustrated, she placed her hand on mine and told me to take my time. I was truly annoyed at the fact that I was having such a hard time catching on. This was not like me. I'm a natural when it comes to school. She leaned over and looked into my eyes. "Repeat after me, '*Tiene los ojos muy sexy.*'"[1] My body immediately relaxed as I began to feel the blood rush from every limb in my body directly to another. I sat up in my seat, "*Usted tiene ojos muy* sexy,"[2] I repeated. "Wonderful," she responded. Then she asked if I could translate it. I knew she said something about eyes and very sexy. "Umm, I have sexy eyes?" "Very good," she responded. "*Usted es muy sexy, quiero que me toques con esas grandes manos de los suyos.*"[3] Just hearing her speak to me in Spanish made my temperature rise. All I could do was stare into her eyes and down her blouse as she leaned over me, holding on to my desk. I imagined standing behind her caressing her supple breast and pulling her hair as I lifted her skirt and . . . "Drake, can you decipher what I just said to you?" I snapped out of my daydream. "I apologize, Ms. DeLeon, I could only make out a few words. I believe you said I am sexy and you want big hands to touch you?"

TRANSLATION

1- He has very sexy eyes

2- You have very sexy eyes

3- You are very sexy. I want you to touch me with those big hands of yours.

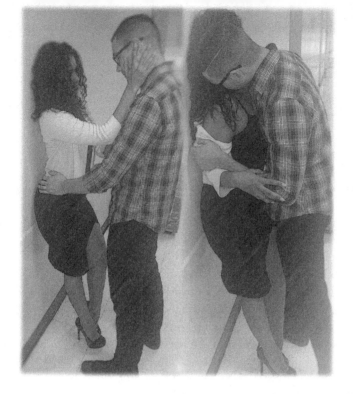

She caressed my face. "Very close, Mr. Hunter. *Levántate, por favor.*[4] I stood up. She took my hand and placed it on her chest, pulled my body close to hers, and said, "I want you to touch me with those big hands of yours, Mr. Hunter."

I couldn't believe that all that I imagined was about to happen. I didn't want to come on too strong. So I dug deep into my Spanish vocabulary and whispered in her ear, "*Su deseo es mi comando.*"[5] I felt her body melt into my arms. I picked her up. She wrapped her legs around my waist as I carried her to the wall by the door. I wanted to make sure it was locked. She stood against the wall massaging her breast and rubbing her hand between her thighs. I went back to her and ripped open her blouse and kissed her neck. She

TRANSLATION

4- Stand up, please

5- Your wish is my command

6- I want you inside me

120

ran her hand through my hair and moaned as I kissed her chest. She reached down and pulled my polo shirt over my head. As I kissed her stomach, I unhooked her bra and slid the straps over her shoulders, revealing her luscious breast. As I made my way back up to her breast, I kissed under each one and slowly slid her right nipple into my mouth. She dug her nails into my back. I lifted her skirt and slid my hand between her legs. As I pulled her panties to the side I could feel how bad she wanted me. She wrapped her arms around my neck and kissed me. I picked her up and sat her on her desk. She reached down into my pants and felt how hard I was. *"Te quiero a ti dentro de mí."*[6] She whispered in my ear. I had no idea what she said, but when she undid my pants, pulled my piece out, and slid it inside, I immediately knew. I moaned as she thrust her hips forward. I moved her hair to the side, kissed her neck, then down her shoulder.

She moved back and forth vigorously like she had her own beat in her head. I wasn't ready to climax and I didn't want her to either. So I laid her back on her desk, lifted her left leg onto my shoulder, grabbed her waist, and slowly allowed her to feel every inch of me flowing in and out of her love. She grabbed my ass, letting me know she wanted me deeper. *"Más adentro!"*[7] she yelled. I picked up her other leg and placed it on my shoulder, grabbed her shoulders, and pounded her deep and hard. She grabbed the side of her desk with one hand and the back of her desk behind her head with the other. *"Sí, papi, sí,"*[8] that's it . . . just like . . . mmm . . . that." She put her legs back around my waist. *"Sentarse*[9], I want to ride you." I loved how she told me what she wanted. That turned me on even more. I sat in her chair, and she straddled me and kissed my chest. She started off slow, rocking back and forth, then she stood a little in her red heels and bounced on me, taking all of me in every time she came down. I ran my fingers through her hair from the back of her neck, then grabbed hold of her hair. She moaned louder. She liked it. I held her tight and fucked back. She looked at me and could tell I was about to climax. She quickly got off of me and slapped my face. It caught me off guard. "What the fuck was that?" I yelled. She walked over to my desk and sat on it. *"No aún no,* not yet, *mi amor.*[10] Now come over here

TRANSLATION

7- Deeper!

8- Yes, daddy, yes

9- Sit

10- Not yet, not yet, my love

121

and eat your dinner!" She had each leg propped up on chairs. I got on my knees and dove in. She tasted like sweet nectar. She grabbed my hair as she grabbed her breast. I wrapped my hands around her ass and squeezed as I pulled her body closer to my face. She wrapped her legs around my neck and pulled my head closer, moving it in the direction that felt good to her. I used my tongue to spell out her name, and with each movement her body trembled. She grabbed me. *"Te quiero dentro de mí."*[11] I slide inside of her wet, warm, waiting . . . She gasped and grabbed me. It felt so good, I couldn't hold back any longer but I didn't want to stop. I pulled back. "Turn around." I bent her over my desk. With every thrust, my desk moved forward. I leaned over her, grabbing her hands as she held on to the edge of my desk. I could hear her voice quaking with each movement I made. "I can't hold it any longer," I whispered in her ear. "Then let me feel you, baby, *déjame sentirte,*"[12] she replied. I released everything that was in me and she screamed with passion and pleasure.

I kissed her back, starting in the middle up to her neck, to her earlobe, her cheek, until I made my way to her lips. She turned around and kissed me so deep, I felt myself rising again. "No, no, no, *papi.* We must save some for another day." I grabbed my pants and pulled them up. She grabbed her clothes and began to get dressed. "Umm, that was absolutely amazing, but what about my grade?" She turned to me. "That's all you can think of right now, huh? Okay, Mr. Hunter, ask me *en Español.*" What? I could barely walk let alone think about what to say . . . "Ummm, *mi grado . . .*" My brain froze as I tried to figure out how to ask this question. "Mr. Hunter, I'm waiting . . . Mr. Hunter, Mr. Hunter. Mr. Hunter!"

I jumped, what the hell! Are you fucking kidding me? I turned and looked around, the entire class was staring at me. "Mr. Hunter. *¿Estás despierto ahora o le gustaría continuar su siesta?*"[13] I shook my head. "I'm sorry can you repeat that?" She looked at me. "¿Estás despierto ahora o le gustaría continuar su siesta?[13] Are you awake now or would you like to continue your nap?" I couldn't believe that it was all just a dream. I heard a few chuckles in the background. How long was I asleep? Was I really asleep or just daydreaming? No wonder I'm not doing well in

TRANSLATION

11- I want you inside me!

12- Let me feel

13- Are you awake now or would like to continue your nap?

122

this class. I can't even focus. Ms. De Leon shook her head. "I'm very disappointed in you, Mr. Hunter. If you care about passing this class, I suggest you see me afterward to discuss your options." I shrugged down into my seat, I was so embarrassed. "*Sí*, professor."

When class ended, I approached her desk. "I apologize, Professor De Leon, I'm usually not like this. I normally get good grades and do well in my classes." She asked me if it was lack of sleep. She really wanted to know what I could do to do better in her class. She suggested tutoring and even gave me a few links to exercises I could study to help improve my grade and understanding. I thanked her for her time, and as I walked toward the door, she stopped me. "Mr. Hunter, one last thing. You seemed to have a smile on your face when you were sleep. Were you having a good dream?" I couldn't lie to her. "Yes, yes, I was." I smiled. She walked over to me toward the door and locked it. "So tell me about it." She ran her hand through her hair and touched my chest with the other. "I see how you look at me, Mr. Hunter. Maybe now, since class is over, your little dream can come true." I dropped my backpack. I couldn't believe this was happening. I guess sometimes dreams DO come true . . .

E nter, scene . . .

The lights were dimmed low in The Spot, a local lounge where the artist and art lovers came to unwind and hear the flows of the local poets in town. Being that I dabbled in a bit of poetry, I loved to come out for a bit of inspiration and networking. Honestly, most of the time I came out hoping to see *HER*. I saw her a few times before. She was rather mysterious, but when she was on the mic, she made her presence known. As the MC approached the mic, he introduced her. "Ladies and gentlemen, coming to the stage to grace you with her authentic lines and sensual flows, Lauryn." She carried herself in such a way that let you know that she had all the confidence in the world. Smooth brown skin, deep brown eyes, pouty and succulent lips, her frame slim but thick in all the right places, her curves flowed like chocolate from a fondue fountain, and legs, oh boy, her legs, thick and defined like she had been running track all her life. She stood about 5'9", but in those heels she was about 6'1". Some may have found her intimidating, but I thought she was sexy, more like a challenge to me. I sat back sipping my cognac—no mixers, I enjoy it neat. I was mellow. I was chill, ready to take in every word she was about to spill.

As her lips parted ways, she spoke the title . . . My mind immediately went to a sensual place. However, as she got into her rhythm and her words flowed like a river, I realized that what she spoke of was deeper than physical. She spoke of the soul, she spoke of the mind, and she touched on the physical, all of these things intertwined. I sat back blown away, wondering what inspired such heartfelt words. I stood to my feet and applauded as loud as I could. I know she couldn't tell mine from anyone else's, but I tried. Who knows, she may have noticed. She walked past me and our eyes met, but only briefly. I was up next. I finished off my drink and I turned to my friend and said, "Hey, man, don't let her leave. I'm not letting her get away once again without meeting me."

The MC came up and gave a little intro to bring me up. He spoke of the last time I was in the building, how I had the ladies thinking and how even some of the guys gave it up. The first time my name was a little nasty, so I cleaned it up for the crowd, something more professional, and something that I could carry with me as an artist. "Ladies and gentlemen, the last time she was on the stage she had you moaning, oh yes, baby. So let's see what kind of feelings she is going to bring out of you tonight. Coming to the stage, Raven the Poet." I tend to be a shy person, but when I'm on the stage and I feel the vibes of the audience, especially when they are engaged, it's like a natural high that can take you away from all the nervousness. Dressed in all black, dark solid black button-fly jeans, black button-down shirt with the sleeves rolled up about a quarter up, black skinny tie, black vest, and clean all black Air Force Ones, I could feel the heat from the lights and the bead of sweat going down my back. I live my life "out loud," if you know what I mean. My low-fade haircut, athletic build (slightly big biceps covered in tattoos), and from one look at me you could tell my main focus in the place was on the ladies. One thing that went through my mind was, "I hope the words I utter tonight lets her recognize me." I began to speak, "The Way She Loves . . . " My mind took me to a place where I could envision every word that came out as I spoke each line, each word. I felt the passion pulsing through my veins and I heard the snaps from the crowd when they came across something with which they could relate. I stumbled across a word or two, once or twice, but the audience reassured me that I was doing good. I heard a lady in the back yell, "Take your time, baby, take your time!" When I finished my poem, I rushed off the stage. I really wanted to see her reaction, and I wanted to know if she was intrigued.

She sat with her friend and I noticed they were engaged in conversation. I didn't want to interrupt, so I walked past but with a slight hesitation. It was one of those passes where you walk by kind of slow, pause, and then proceed. Kind of like it's enough for you to leave them aware of your presence without actually interrupting anything. As I continued by, I heard her say, "So that's the way she loves you huh?" A sly smile came across my face. I turned to her and said, "That's the way I want to be loved." I figured that was a great way to open up a conversation and leave a clue that I was single. She smiled at me and I introduced myself to her and her friend. "Hi, I'm Toni, but I go by Raven." "Hi, I'm Lauryn and this is my good friend Garrett." After the introductions, I asked if my friend and I could join her and her friend. She said yes, and we spent the evening conversing and discussing the talent in the room. As the night lingered on, both our friends decided that they had to go, but we remained and continued talking until the lights were raised and it was officially time to go. I walked her to her car and we exchanged numbers; I told her I really enjoyed the time spent and wanted to get to know her better. She looked into my eyes, smiled, and said, "I guess that's not a bad idea," winked and got into her car. I closed her car door as she rolled down her window. As she prepared to drive off, she made sure to let me know she hoped to hear from me soon and drove off. I stood there with a plastered smile on my face. I couldn't believe this was happening. It was crazy, especially after all of the times I saw her before but never even thought to approach her, let alone get her number.

When I got home that night, I wanted to call her immediately, but what would I say? We did a lot of talking already. So as I paced back and forth in my living room, I decided against it and just locked her number in my phone, went to bed, and figured I'd give it a try another day. I knew she said she hoped to hear from me but so many things ran through my head. What if I say the wrong thing, what if I come off too strong, and what if I this, what if I that . . . I just couldn't get up the nerve to call her for fear of embarrassment.

Days passed and a week went by. Next thing I know, I'm back at The Spot and who do I see? I must admit I was surprised. Looking as lovely as ever, I wanted to rush to her, but I hadn't called her, so I knew I had to play it cool. As she stood by the bar, I walked over and stood beside her, called the bartender over, and said, "Whatever she is having, I got her." Lauryn looked over at me and said, "So is this your way of attempting to make it up to me for not calling?" with a slight laugh. I smiled, and not wanting to get too defensive, I just said, "Well, I figured it was something I should do for a beautiful lady." She smiled and shook her head and grabbed her drink and invited me to her table. Part of me felt like she knew I was digging her and that me not calling her was pure nervousness.

I was surprised she wasn't mad, not like the typical women I usually encounter. You know, the ones that go off and yell, "Oh you couldn't call me but you have yo ass back up in here trying to buy me a drink like you didn't do shit wrong." She was much more poised, very easygoing. She didn't let that become her sole outlook on me as a person or judge that as my character. I think she knew she would see me here anyway regardless of whether I had called or not. Neither of us performed this night, we both just enjoyed the show. I asked what she was doing tomorrow. She said just a day of relaxing, nothing much really, nothing big. I asked her if I could spend some time with her and get to know her outside of this. "Of course, I don't see why not," she responded, "But you may want to give me your number. I'd hate to be waiting for your call and NEVER hear from you until the next poetry night." I couldn't help but laugh as I gave her my number.

So she invited me over so we could spend more time together and get to know each other. From the moment she opened the door, everything between us was like a whirlwind. Let me see, how should I begin? Everything was so innocent just chillin' and relaxin'. She caught my eye and on the fly you figured out my passion. My passion for love without a word spoken. She felt me, she got me, and she understood everything about me. I loved it, it soothed me, and dare

I say it, it grooved me. Day by day went by and she always caught my eye with the little things she did. We talked about her love for kids. Not only did we share the same interests, but we also shared the same passions, and on this one night, in the midst of having fun . . . we kissed. We hung out like true friends do. You get to know me and I get to know you.

We found out that we had mutual friends, so that made it even better and easier to find time to spend . . . together. Now let's go back to this first kiss. I must admit I was out of it and it was somewhat dismissed. See, at this party, I had gotten pretty drunk and she saw an opportunity, into this pool of me she jumped. She climbed on top of me and kissed my lips. I opened my eyes, inside her mouth my tongue slipped. I wrapped my hands around her body and held tight. I couldn't believe that this was happening this very night. I knew I wanted more but I had to get home, and although I was drinking, I safely made it home. I called her up. She said she hated being alone. I hated to leave her there, but after that she wouldn't be alone . . . for long.

Another day passed and I couldn't wait to see her. My heart would race when she'd text can I meet her. I always knew that what we did would be spectacular. It's like being a kid . . . she's running and I'm chasing after her. But it wasn't a chase because I knew that she dug me. She cooked for me and fed me too, it was oh so lovely. A perfect match every time we were together.

She even expressed to me how she liked to make love when there was bad weather. I came to her place and it just so happened to be raining. I walked through the door and our passion needed no explaining. She ripped off my clothes as I ripped hers off too. No need to go all the way into the bedroom, the passion started soon as I walked through the door, clothes flying everywhere and landing all over the floor. To kiss your lips was something oh so divine, I missed your touch and I could tell you missed mine. We made love for hours while listening to slow jams. We lost track of time, but it didn't matter, we were both engulfed in our romance. Over and over we flipped back and forth, forth and back. She liked it this way and I liked it like that. She liked to ride, she liked it from behind, and she also told me she liked it when I was deep inside.

She liked to scream out loud. Not gonna lie, that shit made me proud. She told me it felt good, but usually she doesn't cum. I was

131

then convinced that I would make her feel a big one. I wanted to make sure that her pleasure was secured. She deserved that. She always made sure I felt good. So I wanted nothing less than that.

When I say she was good, I don't mean with just the sex. She took care of me, she always did more, never less. She was my ear or my shoulder to cry on. We laughed together. She showed me things and put me on. Then there came the point when she said those three little words. She told me she loved me and I knew I loved her. I wanted to be around her every moment that I could. To wake up next to her was a morning that was always good. She always made sure that if she could provide it, then I had it. Shit, if I was hungry, she's cooking breakfast with no static. Whether it's first thing in the morning or right after sex, wearing my shirt or butt naked with an apron. Waking up to the smell of pancakes and eggs and a side of sausage, nothing seemed better than what she had to offer.

But see, thing about me is I always play the fool. And even though she truly loved me and her heart was true, I, being me, was always out there looking for an excuse. An excuse not to love her and give myself as I should. All she wanted was all of me, to be enough, and for us to be all good. And by that I mean she wanted to know she was all I needed and that all she gave was everything and more. All she wanted was to be loved completely. All she wanted was the best for me. All she wanted was the passion she gave me.

The passion, the passion I loved so much. The passion she showed from a single touch. The passion she conveyed in a single kiss. The passion that allowed her to be herself and have the best time when we went on road trips. For all that we did and all that we shared, the many nights of loving and the days of taking care. Going above and beyond and singing to me and writing poems. Yet and still I was a coward and could not give my all. And this passion we shared was bound to fall.

She came to me because she noticed my change. This passion, our passion, just wasn't the same. I couldn't give her what she truly wanted from me. A true commitment, for whatever reason, just wasn't for me. So she came to me one night drenched in tears, waiting for me to say the words and confirm her fears.

Sadly I delivered . . . and it hurt her so bad. But little did she know that it truly made me sad. I broke my own heart in the process.

I felt that my decision wasn't the best that I had made. I tried to go back to her, but by that time it didn't matter, it was too late, the decision had been made.

So now I find myself back here at The Spot after telling the abridged version of my romance. I figured I'd never see her again since she knew I came here, this is where we met, poetry . . . our first love, the thing that led to our romance. When she saw me, she didn't even speak. I knew that I hurt her and that our contact would be bleak. They called Lauryn to the stage and I couldn't wait to hear it. She said she hadn't written in a while, but this poem was recently inspired. My heart skipped a beat. I immediately started to perspire. Was it hot in here? Part of my body lost feeling. I felt like I was having a stroke, but it was love taking over, reminding me that what I had with her was no longer.

She spoke . . . The title alone let me know that every word was meant for me. She touched on all the emotions we shared, all the physical, and all the mental . . . no one else compared. As she spoke my heart pounded, as she spoke my palms began to sweat, as she spoke I realized that deep down inside I wasn't done with her yet. Alas, it didn't matter, because I knew she was through. I could only blame me. As she stood on stage I wanted to scream, "I Love You!"

She ended her poem with a question, which forever plagued my world, "Did I touch you?"

Ha, did she touch me? In more ways than one . . . she captured my heart, she inspired my soul, she lifted me up, she encouraged my goals, she made me have fun, she took care of my needs, she made love to me, in every way I was pleased . . . Did she touch me? Did she touch me? Hmm . . . I guess it doesn't matter anymore and I know everything happens for a reason. I'm just blessed to have had an opportunity to spend part of my life with her. Yeah, Baby, you touched me . . . *snap, snap, snap*

End scene . . . fade to black . . .

It was a normal day in the office. I came in at 9:00 a.m., sat down at my desk, and was already ready for my day to be over. "Good morning, Caleb," the cute chick at the desk next to me always spoke (such a sweetheart). I took a deep breath as my computer loaded up for the day. I started to think to myself, damn, how is it that I'm thirty-one and still single? Friends would tell me I was a great catch, 6'1", medium brown skin, light brown eyes. I always kept a clean-cut fade (that is, until I went for the bald look last year). I held two degrees and a great job as an IT technician for a multimillion-dollar company, no kids, and I've been told that I have a nice smile and an award-winning personality . . . I guess these days a man needs more to get a good woman. I really didn't know.

Okay, well, enough of wallowing in my thoughts, time to get this day going. "Hey, everyone, we have a new addition to the IT department!" David, our department manager, stood and announced to our group. Standing next to him was one of the most gorgeous women I have ever seen in a while (well, that actually truly caught my attention). "This is Victoria. She's new to the company and is going to make a great addition to our department. So make sure you make her feel welcome and offer any type of assistance she may need for a smooth start." Victoria stood about 5'1", a smile that could light up a room, deep brown eyes, her outfit hugged every curve on her body (and she had one of those "Coke bottle" bodies). Her hair was cut low, jet-black, you could tell she had some Spanish descent running through her veins from the beautiful shining waves of her hair. She was thick in all the right places, thighs that look like they could break a board if she squeezed tight enough, light caramel brown skin that glistened even under this terrible office lighting. Whoa, I had to shake my head to snap myself out of this; I could only imagine the type of stare that I was giving her, that of a wolf about to attack and feast on a sheep. I'm glad I fixed my facial expression because as I looked back at her I noticed she glanced my way. I couldn't help but smile as she smiled at me.

After the office introduction, I sat back at my desk and continued my workday, but Victoria plagued my mind. I wondered so much about her; was she married, does she have a boyfriend, did she really smile at me or was that just a friendly glance? When lunch rolled around, I wanted to ask her if she wanted to go to lunch with me, but so did like four other guys from the office (go figure). Then I overheard her say, "No, thank you," she was meeting someone for lunch. As she walked out of the door, I saw her get into the car with a dude. Great! I thought, I knew it! Married! Well, there goes all of my hopes and dreams.

I walked over to my best friend Tommy's cubicle to chat about the "new chick" and head out to grab a bite to eat. Upon our return, I didn't even bother looking her way. I wasn't about to get myself all worked up over something that can never happen. Plus, Tommy made a point, never mix business with pleasure. Tommy and I have been friends for over five years and have seen each other through the thick and thin of different relationships. From that point on, the day was dragging by. I really couldn't wait to get out of there. I must have checked the clock about fifty times, but when I checked for the fifty-first time, it was time to go. I packed up my things, shut the computer down, and headed home. When I arrived home, I thought about her again, but reminded myself that it was a lost cause. I walked my dog, cooked myself a frozen dinner, took a shower, and lay down for the evening.

Each day I came in, our eyes would connect. Victoria would speak and I would relish in her ambiance and smile. I kept reminding myself she's taken, don't get excited over nothing. That is, until that day came. David walked in and said, "Hey, team, we have an IT convention coming up in New Orleans in two weeks. Unfortunately, the entire team can't attend; however, the company has allowed six to go. We want to mix up some of our veteran employees with some newbies so they can get the exposure and increase their knowledge. The six going will be Sherry, Caleb, Tommy, Victoria, Michelle, and myself." Stoked, I went over to Tommy's desk, and although we knew we were going for business, we started planning our escape and party plans. I looked back at Victoria as she spoke with Sherry and Michelle. She happened to look up as I was looking over. All I could think about was what I wish I could do with her if only she wasn't taken.

As Tommy and I left for lunch, I glanced over and saw Victoria once again leave to have lunch with her "dude." Tommy nudged me when he noticed me staring in her direction. "C'mon, man, let's go. Stop daydreaming about that girl!" I turned around and met Tommy at his car so we could grab a bite and hurry back to work.

A couple of days passed and I had the pleasure of working with Victoria more. I got the chance to really get to know her. She turned out to be a really cool person, even though she was a 49er's fan (being from Cali). Seahawks for life over here, baby! Nonetheless, she was a blast to be around in the office; she made work worth going to. One afternoon, Tommy and I decided to invite her to join us for happy hour drinks after work. I didn't want to seem too eager, so I asked Tommy if he would ask her. Being the great friend that he was, he did.

"So . . . umm, Victoria, Caleb and I are planning on grabbing some drinks after work, would you like to join us?"

"That is, if your dude is okay with it," I chimed in behind Tommy.

Victoria cut her eyes at me. "Excuse me! If my dude is okay with it? Last time I checked, I was a grown ass woman!" she said with a sly smile.

Tommy laughed. "Man! She told yo ass!" I stood there with the dumbest look on my face (partially blushing, partially shocked, and with a slight grin). In my attempt to pick my face up off the floor, the only thing that came out of my mouth was, "I know, right? Damn! Okay then, bring ya ass!" We all laughed it out and headed back to our desk to finish out the day.

It was about 5:30 p.m. and we met up at a local tavern that wasn't too far from the job. After each of us were a few beers in and finished venting about work, Victoria looked at me with those sexy brown eyes and said, "So earlier you said my dude . . . how do you know I have a dude?" Almost choking on my beer, I caught my breath, but then Tommy jumped in to instigate, "Yeah, homie! How do you know she has a dude?" I slowly glanced over at Tommy and mouthed the words "fuck you" with a big smile on my face. Tommy smiled back.

"Well, I just noticed how he would pick you up for lunch." Victoria turned to me and placed her hand on my wrist. "Well, if you MUST know, first off, that's not a dude. It's a female and she's my best friend." This time Tommy choked on his beer. "That's a chick!" he said. I just smiled and laughed. "Yes! SHE is!" Victoria replied to Tommy.

She then turned back to me, smiling. I must say that moment was the highlight of the evening. We stayed and joked around a little more at Tommy's expense and his reaction to the "dude" being a "woman," then headed our separate ways home.

The three of us hung out a few more times after that. I learned that she is definitely a lady, but she can also hang with the fellas. Which is AWESOME! I also found out that although I was wrong about the "dude" in the car picking her up, she was in a relationship.

As time drew closer for the trip to New Orleans, I got more and more excited. Yeah, she was taken but she was great eye candy and hella fun to be around. She knew football, she talked shit, drank beers, and all while still looking sexy and beautiful (her smile still gets me every time). So I was stoked about chilling with my best friend and new friend during downtime on the trip.

When we arrived at work the next day, David called a brief meeting for the six of us regarding the upcoming trip. We all stood around the conference table waiting for David to come in. As David walked into the room, he said, "Good morning, everyone, I hope you are ready for this upcoming week. I have here everyone's boarding passes. We will be leaving 8:00 a.m. Saturday morning and arriving about 4:30 p.m., which gives us a couple of days to gather our thoughts before we head to the convention on Monday. On Monday, we will meet in the lobby of the hotel at 6:00 a.m. so that we can take the shuttle to the convention center." "So wait! The company is paying for us to spend a couple of extra days in New Orleans?" Tommy interrupted. "Yes Tommy, for all of our dedication and hard work. The company decided to give us a couple of days of r and r before the convention. So thank the company." David replied. "Now back to what I was saying. We should arrive no later than 6:15, maybe 6:20. The first meeting begins at 7:00, so we will have time to grab a quick breakfast just in case you haven't already eaten before we go in." The first thing that came to my mind was, hmmm, a day to chill before the meetings, what can I get into? I looked over at Victoria. She was exactly what I would like to get into.

"Okay, everyone, here's your boarding passes." As David handed out the boarding passes, I hoped that I was seated by Victoria.

"Hey, Victoria, what's your seat number?"

"A3," she replied. "You?"

Damn! I thought to myself. "I'm C4. Who's next to you?"

"I'm B3," David said with a cunning smile on his face. He turned to Victoria and winked. She gave him a half smile with a look of discontent, then turned to me and shrugged. I could tell she was kind of disappointed. I went to Tommy and asked where he was sitting.

"Next to you, homie! D4!" I immediately wondered if he would be willing to help me switch seats with David.

"Hey, man, we're best friends, right?"

"Yeah, what's up? You must want something," he laughed and replied.

"You think you can help me get David to switch out our seats so I can sit next to Victoria?"

"Hell naw, man! I'm not sitting next to David that entire flight!"

I really wanted to sit by her, so I found myself damn near begging. "C'mon, man! Please, first drinks in NO on me, dude, please!"

Tommy looked at me with a side eye, then he looked at Victoria and noticed her look of displeasure as she talked to David. Tommy looked back at me and smiled, "Okay, I got you. Hey! David, can I speak to you for a moment?"

As Tommy pulled David to the side, I walked over to Victoria.

"So are you excited about New Orleans?" I asked.

"As excited as I can be considering it's an IT convention and I'll be spending four hours next to David talking about the convention on the way there."

Our eyes met and she smiled, then she reached up and straightened my collar. Tommy jogged over to us and placed his arms over both of our shoulders. "You owe me TWO drinks, my friend! Looks like you and Victoria will be plane buddies while I listen to David explain in uninterrupted detail what the convention entails this year." My eyes lit up. I hoped that my face didn't show how ecstatic I was. Victoria looked back at me as she got ready to leave the room and head to her desk. "Well, I guess I'll see you later, plane buddy." She laughed and walked out of the room. I couldn't thank Tommy enough.

As soon as I got off of work, I went to look for some new clothes to wear on the trip. Normally I just wear the same ole suits and call it a day, but I couldn't go to New Orleans and spend time around this amazing woman wearing my basics. Part of me wondered why I was putting so much effort into a woman that's taken. But I couldn't help myself. The attraction I felt toward her was so strong and hard to fight. After an evening of getting together my best outfits, I packed for the trip. As I crawled into bed, I found myself thinking about her. Thinking about what I would say, what we could do while out there, if she was thinking about me too . . .

My alarm went off at 4:30 a.m. I hopped in the shower, cleaned up, and got dressed. For the trip down I wore my royal blue polo shirt and loose-fit jeans. I sprayed on my new cologne. It had hints of citrus, pine, cashmere, wood, and leather—a sweet musk, very crisp, not overwhelming. I arrived at the airport at 6:00 a.m. for our eight o'clock flight. We all seemed to have arrived at the same time. I walked over and greeted everyone. As I turned back around, I saw Victoria's car pull up, but it wasn't the best friend with her this time. This time it was clearly a dude, I assumed her dude. I turned back around toward our group quickly so it wouldn't look so obvious that I was staring. Tommy tapped my shoulder. "Hey, there's ya girl Victoria, looks like her dude dropping her off."

"Yeah, I saw that," I replied. All I could think was, DAMN! He's a lucky ass man!

"Hey, guys! I made it! I just knew I was going to be late. He drives slow as hell!" she said, laughing. Victoria walked over and gave everyone a hug; when she got to me, she was slow to pull back as she hugged me. "Mmmm . . . you smell really nice." I don't know if anyone could tell, but I swear I was blushing. "Thank you," I replied.

We checked our luggage curbside and David proceeded to gather everyone. "Okay, ladies and gentlemen, you all are the chosen few to represent our great company. Let's make sure we gather plenty of information to bring back with us." We boarded the plane and I took my seat next to Victoria. She looked up at me and smiled.

"So you ready?" I asked.

"More than you know," she replied.

That reply made my heart race and I had no idea why. Shit, who was I kidding? I knew why. Could it be because I was about to have four hours alone next to undoubtedly the most beautiful woman I've ever laid eyes on? Probably! After we got situated and the crew finished going over their flight speeches, we began talking. We talked about the company, where did I see myself going in the future, how she felt about her new position, how she's adjusting to Seattle compared to being in California. She really opened up to me and she kept me laughing. I think there were a few times where the guy in the seat across from me gave me a bothered look for laughing too loud. I couldn't have cared less though, I was truly enjoying her company.

I finally felt comfortable enough to ask about her relationship, I had to, it was eating me up inside. I needed to know more, I needed to know that she was completely happy and totally satisfied with this man and that I stood NO chance. She looked at me. Her expression changed from a smile to a very serious look.

"Caleb, I need to tell you something, but you must promise me that it stays between us."

My heart raced once again. What was she about to tell me? She's pregnant? She's getting a divorce? I looked into her deep brown eyes and told her, "Of course, you have my word. What's wrong?"

She proceeded to say, "I'm serious, Caleb, I don't talk to or trust many people. I'm a very private person and I normally don't even open up to my coworkers. I keep work and home separate. I DON'T like people knowing or being in my business." At this point I knew that whatever she was about to tell me, I needed to take this and anything else going forward mentioned between us to my grave. I looked her in her eyes. "Victoria, you can trust me. What's on your mind?"

She took a deep breath and placed her hand on my knee. "Well, it's my dude, I don't actually have a dude. The chick that was taking me to lunch, my 'best friend,' is actually my girlfriend." I sat there praying my eyes didn't get big when she revealed her news. I was blown away but not really too surprised. I sat back into my seat and called the flight attendant. I needed a drink. Victoria looked at me. "Dude, are you okay?" It took me a few seconds to collect myself. I tuned back to her and asked, "Well, why didn't you say that before? Oh, and yeah I'm okay, just need a drink. That kinda caught me off guard."

"Well, I didn't say anything before because I don't like people in my personal business, especially people I work with. I'm new to the company and I don't like to be labeled, especially not labeled the new lesbian at the company."

I nodded my head. It made sense. The flight attendant came by. "Yes, sir, what can I get you?"

"A vodka and orange juice please. Victoria, would you like something?"

"Yeah, I'll have the same."

No wonder she was so cool. I guess she was comfortable around us guys because she doesn't like guys. Wait! She doesn't like guys! Shit! She doesn't like guys . . . My heart sank. I looked at Victoria. "I understand completely. Well, who was the guy that dropped you off this morning?"

"That was my brother."

I nodded again. "Oh okay."

"Here you are, sir, ma'am."

As we got our drinks, she sipped hers. I chugged mine and asked for another. The rest of the flight wasn't uncomfortable, but I felt like all hope was gone, forget whether or not she was happy at home. After the drinks I was able to relax again, so I asked her about her girlfriend. She asked me why was I single. I told her that's something I've been trying to figure out myself for the longest. She looked at me, smiling. "Well, you are definitely a very handsome, sexy, smart, and sweet man." She ran her finger down my chest to my stomach. "Oh and I see you work out too, a great package I must say." I felt myself getting hot. I smiled and thanked her. Just as I was about to ask a little more about her situation at home, the plane landed. "Welcome to New Orleans." We toasted with what was left in our glass and finished up our drinks.

When we arrived at the hotel, we got checked in and went to our rooms. All I could think about was my chance missed with her. As I lay in my bed, my phone rang. It was Tommy. "Dude, I thought that plane would never land. I'm starting to think you owe me three drinks now! What are you doing, man? Why so quiet?"

"Nothing, I'm good," I replied.

"You sure?"

"Yeah, yeah, I'm good. I'll meet you downstairs in an hour."

"All right. Oh, and hit up Victoria, see if she wants to come with us."

"Yup, will do!" I hung up and stared at the ceiling. There was a knock at my door. As I opened it, it was Victoria.

"Hey, Caleb, things just didn't seem right after our talk on the plane, you mind if I come in?"

"Sure." She walked past me. She asked if I was okay. I was disappointed but I didn't want her to know. I mean, I understand her being taken. I would have been more shocked if she were single. But damn, she was with a female. I can't compete with that, I thought to myself.

"Naw, you good, I was just a li'l surprised. That's all." She walked over to me. I looked down at her as she came closer. She wrapped her arms around me and hugged me. "Thank you for keeping this between us. It really means a lot to me." She kissed me on the cheek and looked at me. Her eyes were so sincere, I couldn't be upset or disappointed. As she headed toward the door, I asked her about going out for drinks with the group. She declined. "I'm tired from the flight and early morning. I will catch up with you all later." I wanted to ask her to stay here with me.

"Victoria!"

She turned around. "Yeah?"

"I need to be honest with you."

I sat her down and told her how I really felt. About how I thought she was the most beautiful woman I've ever seen, how I needed to be sure everything was good at home, how I wished that I could make her mine. She thought it was flattering and told me how she thought I was cute too. However, that was about it. She wanted to make sure that it was cool for us to still be friends despite everything. Of course, I said yes. She got up to leave once again. And again I called her back.

"Victoria!"

She smiled. "Yes, Caleb."

"Can I get another hug goodbye?" I asked as I sat on the bed. She came over and hugged me, then she gently kissed me on the cheek again, but this time closer to my lips. As she slowly drew back, she kissed me a second time, but this time it was a peck on the lips. It was so soft and sensuous, her lips were like soft pillows against mine.

As she looked deep into my eyes, I wrapped my arms around her waist. She grabbed my head and kissed me harder. She kissed me with such conviction like it was something she had to get out of her system. Our tongues danced. I grabbed her ass and pulled her even closer, as if I were trying to merge us into one person. She bit my bottom lip, then she pushed away from me.

"I . . . um . . . I gotta go, Caleb. I'm sorry. I gotta go." And like that, she left. I jumped in the shower to cool off, got dressed, and met Tommy, Sherry, Michelle, and David downstairs.

"Hey, where's Victoria?" David asked.

"She said she was tired from the flight and would catch up with us later," I replied.

"Oh, okay, great! Just didn't want her feeling left out."

Tommy turned to me. "Dude, what did you do to her?" He said, laughing. "You must have scared her away, talking that talk on the flight here." I looked at Tommy with a grin, trying not to show all over my face what had just happened in the room.

"Naw, man, I called her and she just said she was tired and would catch up with us later. I don't know."

Tommy shrugged and we went to the French Quarter and had a few drinks and grabbed a bite to eat. All I could think about was Victoria and her lips. Tommy could tell something was on my mind but didn't probe since our other coworkers were out with us. I excused myself early. "Hey, guys, I've had a long morning, I'm gonna turn in early." I went back to my room and went to sleep thinking about Victoria.

The next morning, we all met up for beignets and coffee in the French Quarter. After breakfast we spent the day out sightseeing and shopping around as a group. While in this one little shop, Victoria found a Mardi Gras mask that caught her eye. She tried it on and looked in the mirror. She instantly fell in love. I walked over to the shopkeeper and asked how much for the mask. I paid for it, walked up behind Victoria, and whispered in her ear, "It's yours." She turned around and said she couldn't let me pay for it. She went into her purse to pull out cash. I politely pushed her purse away.

"No, no need for that, it's a gift for you to remember this trip to New Orleans."

She smiled and thanked me as we walked out of the shop. After about four hours of in and out of shops and on tours, I was exhausted, so I headed back to my room.

Not even thirty minutes after lying down, I received a call from Victoria about hitting Bourbon Street later on that night. Of course, I couldn't say no. So I took a short nap, showered, and got ready for an evening out. Even though I knew it would be warm out, I still wanted to make a great impression, so I put on my classic button-fly jeans, a black muscle shirt, and form-fitting button-down black shirt. I freshened up with a little cologne and met Tommy and Victoria in the lobby.

We hit a few jazz clubs, had a nice dinner, and enjoyed the music with a few drinks. Once we were nice and loose, we went to a couple of dance spots. With each dance between Victoria and me, everything between us just felt right, it felt natural. Her smile, when she looked in my eyes. It could have been the drinks, but with every touch and gesture, part of me wanted to believe she wanted me.

"Let me know if I'm getting too touchy-feely with you. I tend to do that when I've been drinking. I also tend to flirt a lot," Victoria said as she smiled at me, laughed, and winked. "Oh no, you're fine. Just be yourself and have fun. We're in New Orleans!" I replied. While thinking to myself, of course! It's the drinks, oh well, I'm going to enjoy every touch and flirt while I can. We stopped off at Tropical Isle and we each got a shot and drank hand grenades. Although we had to be up early, we still

partied like there wasn't a care in the world. Once we made it to the third club, I looked over at my watch. Victoria placed her hand over my watch.

"Why are you watching the time? Just relax and enjoy yourself. Even if we are exhausted in the morning. I promise you, it WILL be worth it!"

How could I resist that? So I disregarded the time and danced the night away with this beautiful woman.

As we lifted out glasses to take our last shot, I could tell I was lit. I was sitting there hoping I could remember my way back to the hotel. I looked over at Tommy, who seemed pretty inebriated, talking to some chick on the dance floor. Then I glanced over at Victoria and she looked just as drunk as I was. I knew then that I needed to sober up and get us back to the hotel safely.

"Hey, you ready to head back?" I asked Victoria. She nodded, so I grabbed her hand and walked over to Tommy to see if he was ready to head back.

"Hey, we are about to head back, you ready, man?" Tommy was deep into his conversation and the club was loud. I tapped him on the shoulder.

"Hey, man! You ready?"

He turned around. "Naw, man, I'm good. I'm gonna stay here with her. I'll see you back at the hotel." I gave him some dap and Victoria and I left out.

The night was amazing. I didn't want it to end. But I knew that all good things must come to an end. I walked Victoria to her room. We laughed and talked about our evening. I opened her door for her. "You in a rush to go back to your room?" she asked.

"Umm, no, not at all," I replied.

"Great, because as much as I've been drinking, there is no way I would be able to unzip this dress on my own."

I slowly closed the door. "Oh . . . umm . . . yeah, of course. I can give you a hand."

She smiled at me. "Thanks, babe."

I'll admit I was nervous, so I hung back for the official okay. I mean, after all, she did belong to someone else and what were the chances that our lips would find each other again. She turned back to me. Her light brown skin was glistening from the humidity outside. She smelled like a freshly picked flower, with morning dew and a hint of jasmine, a combination that set my loins on fire.

I slowly unzipped her dress. Everything inside of me said no, don't do it! But I couldn't control my body and couldn't live with myself if I hadn't tried. So I did . . . I gently kissed her back, right below her neck. I waited for her to jump forward, slap me, or pull away, but she didn't, she caressed her breast with her left hand and grabbed my head with her right. Her hands slowly slid down the side of my face as I kissed her neck and down her shoulder.

I sat on the edge of the bed. She came over and climbed on top of me. She looked into my eyes and kissed me. I ran my hand from the small of her back to her ass. She kissed my chest down to my stomach, then slowly stood to her feet. She walked over toward the dresser, picked up her mask from earlier, and placed it on her face.

151

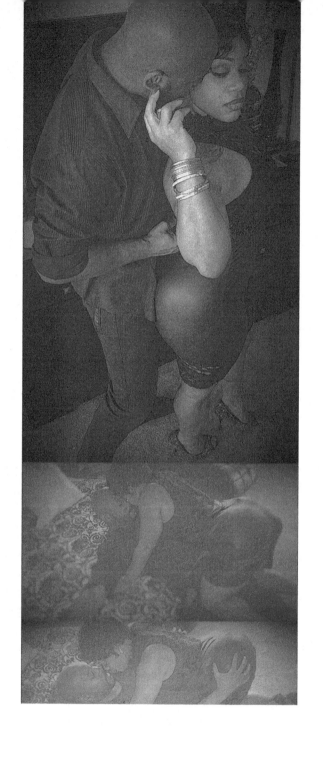

"Thank you again for the mask. So what do you think?" she asked.

I lay there in disbelief. I couldn't believe this was happening. She was so beautiful and the mask added a bit of mystery, a bit of seductiveness, if you will.

"No response? Does that mean you don't like it?" Victoria said with a slight laugh.

"Oh, my bad! No, it's actually very sexy." I walked over to her. As I came close to her, she slowly kissed me once again. She grabbed my hand and led me over to the chaise lounge. She lay back and I climbed between her legs. I kissed her inner thigh and ran my tongue down her thigh to her waiting yoni. I slid the dress off her shoulders, over her breast, and to her waist. By this time I was hard, ready to give her every piece of me. I kissed those soft lips once again, and as I slid my tongue into her mouth, I slid my finger into her warmth . . . She moaned with pleasure and clinched my back. I kissed her deep and passionately, placed my hands on her waist, grabbed hold tight, and pulled her close to me. I knew she could feel my king pressed against her warmth. She pulled her body closer to mine. I could tell she wanted me inside her.

She unzipped my pants, and grabbed my bulging lingam. "Wait . . . " I grabbed a condom from my back pocket (I stay prepared), slid it on, pulled her panties to the side, and slid it inside her dripping wet yoni. She gasped as I thrust as if I was taking her breath away. Victoria grabbed my head, looked in to my eyes, and pulled my mouth to her waiting tongue. I clinched her bottom lip between my teeth, slowly released, and sucked her lip as I picked her up and laid her on the bed. She ripped my shirt off. I pulled her dress down her legs and off her body.

"Turn over," I said. She got on her knees with her ass in the air. I ran my tongue from her shoulder to her back and kissed down the small of her back until I was right above her luscious, round, soft ass. I pulled her black lace thong off and dove in face first. I wanted to devour all of her. I licked her wet yoni. She trembled as I licked from her clit to her ass. I pulled off my pants and boxers, positioned her ass up as she lay her head on the bed. I slid my king in easy, then gave her a deep thrust while grabbing her hips, squeezing as I dug deep inside her. She moaned louder as I dove in. I grabbed her shoulders so I could get a deeper push

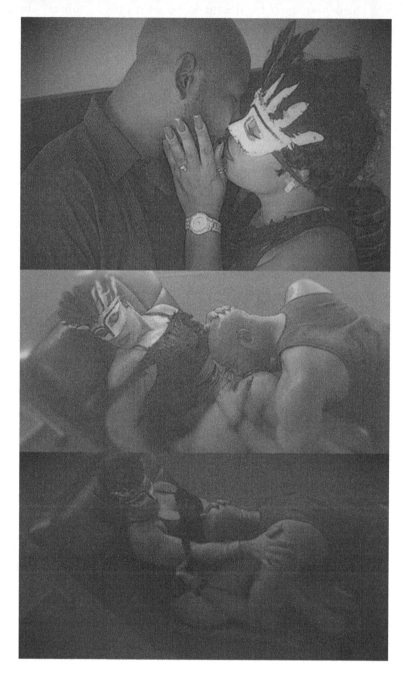

inside. She let out a scream of pleasure. I leaned over and kissed her back. I didn't want her to climax just yet. I turned her over, grabbed her by her thick thighs, and pulled her close to me. I leaned in and kissed her neck, her lips . . . her chest until I reached her right breast while I massaged her left. She rubbed my head and scratched my neck, then she pulled me to her so she could feel my lips against hers. She sucked on my lip as she reached for my king and put it back inside her.

I stroked slow and steady, making sure she felt my every movement. She moaned in my ear as she grabbed the back of my neck with one hand and her breast with the other. The deeper I went the louder she moaned and the more she dug her nails into my back. My slow strokes turned to deep thrusts as my sweat dripped from my forehead to her chest. She wiped my brow. I lifted her legs, pulled out, and glided my tongue into her warmth. I licked every inch and vibrated my tongue over her clit. I placed my index finger inside and played with her G-spot. The faster I licked, the harder and faster I fucked her using my fingers like they were my king. She fucked back with intensity, going harder and harder, moaning louder and louder until she climaxed. But we weren't done.

She looked at me as I raised my head. My mouth was drenched. "I want your king inside my mouth." She stood at the edge of the bed. I lay on my back and motioned for her to climb on top of me. She climbed on me and kissed me once again. She slid down and placed my still hard lingam in her mouth. She licked and sucked with such conviction and passion like my king was a melting popsicle and she wanted to catch every drop. It felt so good, it was almost overwhelming. My toes curled. She grabbed my arm so I couldn't move (and I liked the restraint). I grabbed the edge of the bed with my other hand. "Baby, baby, oh shit, Victoria, damn, fuck!" I couldn't even begin to make sense of the words coming out of my mouth. I grabbed her hair. She looked up at me and ran her tongue from the shaft to the head, kissed the tip, then took all of my king into her mouth. My toes clinched. I grabbed the bed and exploded. She climbed on top of me as I lay limp, kissed my neck, and asked me, "How long before I can make you cum again?" I looked at her, and although every ounce of me was drained, I couldn't get enough of her.

"No, I want to make you cum again," I said. I motioned for her to climb on my face. She rode my tongue and I instantly began to rise again as she looked down at me while massaging her breast and biting her lip. She climbed off and got on her knees in the middle of the bed, I got up and pulled her to the edge of the bed. She reached between her legs and grabbed my king and put it inside,

"You think you can make me cum again?"

"Hell yeah!" I replied.

I started slow, bending over her back to massage her clit and kiss her neck. As she moaned with pleasure, I planted my feet on the floor and held her tight. I slapped her ass as she moved back and forth on me. I watched as her ass clapped on my king as she rocked and moaned. I grabbed her shoulders and dug deep inside her until I felt every inch of me go in. She screamed with pleasure as I hit her spot. She grabbed the bed and buried her head in the sheets so the people next door couldn't hear her scream. I held her tight as I felt her clinch my king with her warmth. I slapped her ass, grabbed her hips, and gave her all of me. She screamed. We climaxed . . . together. I fell to the bed as she lay next to me, trembling with pleasure and aftershocks from her massive orgasm. I caressed her body.

"Oh shit! What time is it?' I asked.

She looked at her phone. "It's 5:00 a.m.! Oh shit!"

"We have to be at the lobby at six!" I grabbed my clothes and started getting dressed. As I headed to the door, she came over to me. "Wait!" She kissed me deep and passionately, then she caressed my face, looked into my eyes, and whispered in my ear, "As much as I wish this wasn't the last time . . . what happens in New Orleans, stays in New Orleans . . ." I smiled and walked out the door. Even though I knew this would never happen again and I couldn't tell anyone about it, I was content knowing that I wasn't alone when it came to the attraction.